THE PEAKS

THE

PEAKS

BASED ON A TRUE STORY

Jill Delee Reed

First paperback edition August 2021

Book design by Glen M. Edelstein, Hudson Valley Book Design

ISBN 978-1-7376348-0-5 (paperback)
ISBN 978-1-7376348-1-2 (eBook)

For Cheryl Peak Taylor – the last of the "Mopeakans."
and
In loving memory of my mother, Ginny.

THE PEAKS

I

January 30, 1949

RUSSELL WAITED. HE'D waited like this before, three times before, but this time just felt different – it was taking too long. He sure hoped Edna was alright. People had told him not to marry her. "She's crazy" they said, "She'll never have children." But he married her anyway; he loved her. And now here they were, having their fourth baby!

He sat fumbling with his hat, holding it by the rim and turning it nervously around and around. He stood and paced, then sat back down. Russell glanced around, down the hall, and out the large windows trying to find something to occupy his mind. Hospitals were nerve-racking and they smelled funny; they were almost eerie. And he couldn't help but notice how terrible the paint job was and the ugly, dull color that did nothing to help the dreary mood of a place most people didn't want to be. Russell had spent years as a painter and he would have not only done a perfect, quality paint job, he would have convinced them to choose a better color.

It was killing him – all this waiting. He hated it. Hours passed. He tried whistling to ease his nerves. Russell would whistle all day long at his store while he worked making his fishing rods. Just a few months ago he finally made the jump from making rods in his garage in his spare time to opening his own shop. It took courage to quit his job as a painter; he was one of the best in Pasadena and with the economy in California there was always plenty of work for Russell to provide for his family. But Edna believed in him and encouraged him endlessly, "You're talented and a hard worker," she would tell him, "You'll never be satisfied d oing w hat y ou t ruly l ove i n t hat s illy o l' garage!" His mind pictured all his finely hand-crafted glass fishing rods lined up neatly against the wall. He loved the feel of them forming in his hands and he loved the way they felt as he tested their flexibility. He spent every day except Sundays in his store: *Russ Peak's Glass Rods of Distinction*. It was a great store and was the one thing that kept *him* from going crazy. He chuckled to himself at the thought.

His mind was instantly swept back to Edna and he wondered for the hundredth time if she was alright. And what about the baby? *Dear God, let this one be a boy*, his mind pleaded. He already had three daughters. The Peak name was going to become extinct. Unless...unless this one was a boy. This was it for Russell and Edna; four children – it was a miracle for sure! *Dear God, what's one more tiny miracle for me? Huh? I've never asked for much. But this...this is something I really, really want.*

Russell's silent prayer was interrupted by the sound of footsteps. He looked up, then stood when he realized it was Edna's doctor walking toward him. Greeting him with a handshake Russell excitedly asked, "How's Edna? How's the baby? Tell me Doc, I gotta know, is it a boy?"

"It's a boy," Edna's doctor said, but with no enthusiasm.

Russell sensed something was wrong, his voice quivered as he asked, "Edna, is she..."

The doctor quickly interrupted to put Russell's mind at ease, "She's fine. Fine, Mr. Peak, she did terrific."

"That's GREAT then! Great…" Russell's voice trailed off as he noticed the grim expression still on Doctor Klein's face. *Why doesn't Doctor Klein seem happy for me?* The baby was a boy, and he knew how much Russell hoped for a boy; he had delivered the three girls.

"Mr. Peak, sit down for a moment." Doctor Klein gently put his hand on Russell's shoulder and motioned toward the chair, sitting himself down next to Russell. Leaning toward him and in a somewhat hushed tone, Doctor Klein said, "Mr. Peak, I'm real sorry for this, but we think your boy is a mongoloid."

Russell stared blankly at Doctor Klein for a moment, letting his words sink in. "A mongoloid?" Russell could barely say the word. "But isn't that one of those retarded kids? I…I don't understand," he stammered. "Edna has problems for sure but how could this happen?" Russell searched Doctor Klein's face for answers. He felt confused and didn't even know what questions to ask.

"Russell, I've known you and Edna for a long time and I believe this can happen to anybody. It seems to be a random kind of thing. It doesn't seem to be genetic, but we just don't know much about it," Doctor Klein attempted to reassure Russell. He leaned in even closer to Russell and lowered his voice to a near whisper, "All we know is that mongoloids are very difficult. They can't function in society and they…" There was a long pause as Dr. Klein looked straight at Russell before continuing, "People don't take this kind of baby home. You'll be a lot better off to put him in an institution. That's where they belong." Doctor Klein again put his hand on Russell's shoulder as he stood, adding, "A nurse will get the baby and transport it for you to make it easier on the both of you," then turned and walked down the hall.

Russell felt sick. He dropped his head down into his hands and rubbed his bald spot and squeezed his eyes shut. *How could this be?* His breathing became labored as his stomach seemed to tighten. It felt as if the hall were wrapping around him like a boa constrictor, squeezing tighter and tighter. He gasped for air as he remembered seeing a mongoloid several years ago in a department store. They looked funny, different, strange. They didn't talk right and had such odd habits and behaviors. All three of his daughters were born just fine, what happened?

Suddenly the boa loosened its grip and Russell had a tremendous urge, no *need* to see Edna. She was so smart; she had graduated magna cum laude from the University of Minnesota. She would be able to help him understand. He started to walk down the hall, his legs regaining desperate strength with every stride. He began to run, shouting out her name, "EDNA! EDNA!" A nurse pointed to a room just down the hall and to his left.

Russell tried to enter the room quietly but was far too strained to succeed. Once inside Russell first saw two other mothers in their beds and apologized for his sudden entrance into their room, "I beg your pardon, I'm Edna's husband, Russell," he said as he glanced further to his right to be sure he was in the right room.

There was his beautiful Edna, sitting up slightly in her bed and holding a very pink and very tiny baby in her arms. Her petite frame looked so small in the oversized hospital gown, and in spite of looking a bit tired, her dark brown eyes were amazingly bright. She smiled softly at him and he gripped his hat tightly as he walked slowly toward her.

"Russell, you have a son now!" she said.

Does she know? Russell wondered. *Certainly Doctor Klein told her.* But she didn't seem to hold this baby any differently than she had held the girls.

Edna gazed down into the baby's face and smiled at it as she adjusted the blue blanket he was tightly wrapped in. Russell stared at her, uncertain of what he should do. Then he noticed her tear-stained cheeks. She knew.

"Hi Honey Girl," he said as he gently kissed Edna on the forehead and sat down on the edge of the bed. "Doc said you did real good." He paused, hoping she would say something, but she simply looked deep into his eyes.

After an awkward moment, Edna asked, "Darling, do you want to hold him?"

Russell stood quickly, shocked by the proposal. He hadn't even looked at it yet. He didn't want to look at it.

With a shaky voice and without looking at the baby, Russell said, "Doc says he's a mongoloid, Edna. He…he says we should put him into one of those institutions. He says it's the best thing – for all of us." Russell nervously pointed at the open doorway and added, "There's a nurse coming to get him for us. She'll…she's going to… Doc said the nurse will take him for us." Russell's gaze fell to the floor and he nodded slightly as he said, "Doctor Klein said it's what we should do."

"Oh Russell, since when have you done what people have told you to do?" Edna said with an almost flirty twinkle in her eye.

She had a point. But he was way over his head with this. He had become accustomed to dealing with Edna's problems; there were treatments that helped her and for the most part they had an ordinary life together. There would never be anything ordinary about their life together again if they took this…this strange baby home. It was retarded. He didn't love it. He *couldn't* love it. *Why did God do this to me? Where is the son I prayed for – to carry on the Peak name? Am I being punished for something?*

Edna's voice broke through his thoughts, "Russell darling, just come look at him. He's so very cute."

Russell gazed down at the baby in Edna's arms. His eyes glazed over, and he couldn't see its face through the blurriness. He blinked to hold back the inevitable, but despite his best efforts, a tear fell onto the baby's face. Russell pulled a handkerchief from his pocket and dabbed at his wet eyes.

Then Russell's vision cleared. He stared down at a tiny pink face with dark hair, a button nose and sleepy eyes that seemed too far apart, but only slightly. A tiny hand suddenly poked up just past the blanket he was wrapped in. It was the tiniest, chubbiest hand he'd ever seen, and the pinky finger bent inward slightly. It was a unique feature, so cute on a hand so small.

Russell chuckled for a brief moment before a flood of emotions overtook him all at once; grief over the loss of the son he had hoped for, joy for the presence of the son he had before him. Russell sobbed for a moment, not even concerned about the other women in the room who were undoubtedly looking at him. He put his big, rough hands around the baby's head and sobbed, "My little son."

Edna reached up and gently stroked her husband's drooping shoulders. "I love you," she said soothingly, through her own tears.

Russell stood suddenly, sensing the presence of someone else near. An older, grey-haired nurse stood at the foot of Edna's bed. She stared, coldly, at the baby in Edna's arms. She spoke in a flat, unemotional voice, "I was told to come for the child and take it for you." After staring at the two tear-stained parents she added, "It's better this way you know. These babies don't belong in regular society," she said pointing at Russell and Edna's baby boy.

Something sparked in Russell's heart. "We're taking him home Edna," he stated matter-of-factly as he took his handkerchief and wiped his eyes thoroughly. Replacing the handkerchief in his pocket, he turned to the nurse and said, "No child of Russ Peak's is going to be in an institution," his piercing blue eyes stared straight at her and he let his words hang in the air. She stared back with indignation and parted her lips slightly as if to say something, but instead gave a small grimace and curtly walked out of the room.

Finding new strength and courage Russell turned to Edna and lovingly stroked her shoulder-length brown hair with his hand and began to think out loud: "We'll just have to figure this thing out. We'll take him to another doctor and get another opinion; maybe they're wrong, or maybe there are treatments." He shrugged his shoulders and continued, "I'm sure we can manage to deal with his problems. It's good the girls came first, they can help. Virginia is almost 11 now, she's very responsible and smart, she'll be a second mother on your bad days Edna. We'll manage. We'll manage," Russell repeated, trying to convince himself as well.

He sat down once again, this time allowing Edna to place the baby into his arms. He held the baby's tiny hand and put his cheek against the baby's cheek. Taking in a deep breath he became excited about the prospects of raising a boy and said, "Awe, heck, maybe I can even teach him to make fishing rods and he can help me out at the store. Right?" he said with a nervous laugh.

He and Edna sat and looked at their new baby for a long time. Russell finally handed the baby back to Edna and stood. "We'll name him David Russell, just like we had talked about if the baby turned out to be a boy."

2

May 1949

DAVID HAD A bad cough and Edna was getting worried. She looked at her baby boy lying in his crib in the corner of their bedroom. As she paced the floor, he began to cough wildly again, gagging himself and spitting up all over his freshly changed sleeper. She gently picked him up and stroked his tiny head, soothing him with her voice, "Darling baby David…Mommy loves you." He began to cough again and that was it, she had had enough. Edna walked quickly to the telephone table and dialed the store phone number. "Russell come home quickly, I need the car to take David to the doctor."

As she tried to drive calmly to the office of their family doctor, Edna looked over at three-and-a-half month-old David in his little basket. *Why won't that awful cough just please quit?* She hated seeing her tiny baby so tortured. The funny thing about it was that baby Davie didn't even seem to mind. He was so good natured. He would cough and cough and the person having fits about it all was Edna. After a fresh coughing spell he would look up at her with a red face and smile.

Doctor Peterson was alarmed as well after examining David and sent Edna and the baby to Doctor Shaw, a pediatrician in the valley. Doctor Shaw gave David a blood transfusion using Edna's blood and 2000 units of penicillin. He also suspected an enlarged thymus, therefore ordering x-rays, which the x-rays confirmed, and Edna was told that David needed radiation therapy.

"Mrs. Peak, has anyone ever said anything else about your baby's health?" Doctor Shaw asked as Edna redressed David.

Edna's heart jumped, fearful of what he was referring to. She and Russell had come to believe over the last few months that their baby boy was perfectly normal. He was so alert and strong – certainly he was just fine and Doctor Klein had simply been mistaken.

"Yes, when he was born, my doctor thought he might be a mongoloid," Edna hated having to admit.

"Well, after examining David I would have to agree that it is a possibility. I think he shows definite signs of mongolism," Dr. Shaw said, trying to be as sensitive as possible.

Edna wanted to run as fast as she could out of the office. She didn't want to address an issue that was only a possibility any way and leaving as quickly as possible would put an end to any further discussion. Edna finished dressing David and asked, "Do I need to make another appointment to come back?"

"I would like David to have two radiation treatments each week for four consecutive weeks," Doctor Shaw said, then advised her to get another opinion from a Doctor Ryan regarding David's *other* condition. She thanked him kindly and walked back into the waiting room. After making the necessary appointments she walked back to their Chrysler De Soto sedan, a lovely car she and Russell had given themselves for Christmas just before David was born. Their life was going so perfectly, why did these doctors have to ruin their happiness with all this talk about mongolism?

Driving home she felt in a daze. "What would she tell Russell? Of course she would inform him about the blood transfusion, the x-rays, the needed radiation treatments – all of which was going to cost quite a sum of money, but would relieve Russell's worry over David's cough. But should she tell him what Doctor Shaw had said at the end of the exam? Russell had become so hopeful. She had too. She felt as if her heart were breaking all over again. Maybe it would be better to spare Russell the worry, after all Doctor Shaw could be wrong. *That's what I'll do, I'll get another opinion from the other doctor and I'm sure it will all work out just fine in the end. Russell doesn't need to know.*

*   *   *

Edna looked at David in his little basket as she once again drove to another Doctor appointment. It had been two and a half months since she had taken him to Doctor Shaw and David had finished his radiation treatments. His cough still lingered and Edna thought it was peculiar it was lasting so long, a fact she didn't want to admit simply because anything out of the ordinary could point to an abnormality. In the middle of David's treatments, she had seen another doctor who said he didn't think there was enough evidence of mongolism. It had given her hope! But today she was nervous. She was on her way to Doctor Ryan's office who, apparently, knew a little more about mongolism than the other doctors who had seen David.

Edna was becoming adept at going through the motions at a physician's office: check in at the front desk, wait. Follow the nurse to the examination room, undress David, wait. Let the doctor poke, prod, and stare and then wait nervously for him to say something. This time was no different so far.

"Well Mrs. Peak…there is no doubt in my mind that your son is a mongoloid" Doctor Ryan broke the silence in such an abrupt and matter-of-fact way. This took Edna a bit by surprise and his words hung in the air like damp laundry on the line to dry. She had heard similar words, but this time the words "no doubt" left her speechless. Her skin suddenly felt tight and she wanted to refute it, but before she could, Doctor Ryan continued, "He shows all the clinical signs: a round face, almond-shaped eyes, small ears, heavy eyelids, protruding tongue, short bent pinky finger, one line across the palm, and a tendency to double-jointedness." Amid feeling overwhelmed, Edna was annoyed that Doctor Ryan would rattle off a list in such a way, like David was nothing more than a curiosity that fit a particular description. The very same list contained many of the things Edna found most endearing about David. "I'd like my associate, Doctor Harvey, to take a look at David if that's alright with you Mrs. Peak?" Edna managed to nod and then regretted the permission as soon as he left the room. But then perhaps Doctor Harvey would disagree with Doctor Ryan's opinion.

Edna could hear footsteps and then two men's voices outside the closed door to the room where she and David sat waiting. She wondered if they were talking about David and if so, what were they saying? Was Doctor Ryan convincing Doctor Harvey that David was a mongoloid before Doctor Harvey could form his own opinion? Then Edna heard a female laugh. *Why would someone laugh? Are they making fun of my son?*

The door opened suddenly which startled Edna and cut off her thoughts. A rather large man walked in and held out his hand to Edna. "Hello, I'm Dr. Harvey." He shook her arm with such force she felt it yank at her shoulder. Immediately Edna thought he seemed rude and unfriendly, but she quickly put her mind in check, knowing that at times she was prone to be a bit paranoid. He stooped down and looked at David, picking up David's hand in his. "Well hello there little man, it's very nice to meet you." Edna watched as he turned David's hand over and studied it. She looked down at David's hand and saw exactly what Doctor Ryan had mentioned – a single crease straight across his palm. Funny she had never noticed before.

Doctor Harvey stood and simply said, "Yes, there's no doubt about it" and turned to Doctor Ryan, said something in a low voice that Edna couldn't hear. She looked down at David who smiled at her and coughed. "How long has he had that cough Mrs. Peak?" Doctor Harvey asked as he opened the door to leave.

"Almost three months."

He glanced at Doctor Ryan, nodded his head slightly and said to Edna, "It was very nice to meet you and your charming little chap."

Edna's face flushed. She felt hot in her short-sleeved cotton summer dress. *How could he come in here, give David a quick look-over and then proclaim he knows David is a mongoloid? And then pretend to be kind! How dare he!*

During the drive home Doctor Ryan's words haunted her. "No doubt about it." She couldn't stop saying those words over and over in her mind. She began talking out loud to David as if he could understand. "Maybe we should get another opinion, I mean, we've only seen a half dozen or so doctors and they did not all agree. One said there was not enough evidence of mongolism and now today Doctor Ryan said there is no doubt." Edna's eyes glazed over, and her chin began to quiver. She gripped the steering wheel tightly and fought back her tears. She could not deny the things Doctor Ryan had noticed, they were all present and all true, she could see them herself. And David was in fact different from her three daughters. Quite different in some areas. But still. Maybe she would ask her friend, Dorothy, whom she would recommend she take David to. Maybe… her thoughts trailed off for the moment as she glanced over at David who smiled his bright smile at her and cooed. "Oh, how I love you so, darling David. I hate dragging you from doctor to doctor." Edna searched her soul. "It doesn't feel right." Edna made a firm decision – no more doctors, no more opinions. It was time to accept it: David was a mongoloid.

Now all she had to do was go home and tell Russell.

*   *   *

Russell walked in through the door at the back porch just past 9:00 that evening. He worked late sometimes. On one occasion Edna awoke in the middle of the night to find that Russell's side of the bed was still empty. She called the store to discover he was still there, working on a special-order rod. He was shocked when she informed him that it was two thirty in the morning. He had completely lost track of time.

Edna was sitting up in bed reading when Russell entered the room. He leaned over and, giving Edna a kiss, Russell absent-mindedly inquired, "How was your day Honey Girl?" but strolled out of the room in the midst of Edna's reply. Edna could hear him in the kitchen, most likely making himself a sandwich. *He must have something on his mind to be so preoccupied, however, it must be something good because he's whistling, which is something he does when he's cheerful* Edna thought. She had to figure out how to approach him with Doctor Riley's statement about David. Russell was in such a wonderful mood; would that be helpful or would the news only squash his spirits? Edna thought maybe she should wait until tomorrow. But tomorrow he would be up early and off to the store and she might not even see him.

Edna walked into the kitchen where Russell was just finishing assembling his sandwich. "Russell, I really need talk to you about baby David," she said, determined to simply get to it. Awkwardly she continued, "I took him to a doctor this afternoon that Doctor Shaw had told me a few months ago he wanted David to go and see." She waited for a reply. Nothing. Fumbling nervously with her fingers she continued, "He looked David over and then had his associate, a Doctor Harvey, look him over also. I didn't care for Doctor Harvey, he was rude and uncaring."

"Why did you have them look at him then? I thought Doctor Shaw was satisfied that his cough was improving, and his thymus had responded well to the radiation." Russell walked into the dining room and sat down to eat his sandwich with Edna following and taking a seat across from him.

"They weren't looking at his cough. Not exactly."

Russell looked up at her with his mouth quite full and managed to strangle out the words, "What were they looking at then?"

Everything all came tumbling out now and Edna felt some relief to unload it. "Doctor Shaw had mentioned a few months ago, when I first took David in because of his cough, that he thought there was a possibility that David was indeed a mongoloid baby. But he wanted me to get the opinion of his friend, Doctor Ryan. He said Doctor Ryan knew more about it than he. I didn't want to unnecessarily worry you about it, so I didn't tell you. I was hoping he would refute it. But he didn't. Doctor Harvey, the rude one, didn't refute it either, Russell." She looked down for a moment. The silence was unbearable. Was Russell upset with *her* or with the diagnosis? "I hope you aren't angry with me for not telling you," she said quietly.

Russell had quit chewing. He sat, staring at Edna. His eyes were thoughtful, not angry. He managed to swallow and after silence that lasted for what seemed to be forever, he very slowly and thoughtfully said, "Well, dear, we were told this before. Maybe we should get another opinion." He put his sandwich down on the plate and sat silent again.

"No Russell. I think it's true." Edna's eyes began to mist as she said, "I didn't want it to be true as badly as you don't want it to be true. But that can't change the things that I can see with my own two eyes. Russell, he has all the characteristics of mongolism – his eyes, his tongue, and as both doctors pointed out today, he has only one crease on the palm of his hands. Even his bent pinkie finger is an attribute of mongolism." Edna began to cry, and Russell came to her and knelt at her knees. Taking his handkerchief from his pants pocket, he dabbed gently at her eyes.

"Darling, don't cry." He held her trembling hands in his and asked, "Did these doctors say anything about treatments?"

"Yes," Edna said, so quietly Russell could barely hear her. "They said there are a few different treatments we can do but they are unsure if they will help him to recover and be a normal boy." That was all they really wanted for David. They just wanted him to have a long and normal life.

3

January — June 1950

EDNA SAT IN the waiting room of her doctor's office. David was now nearly one year old, and he could almost sit alone. She thought about how grateful to God she was for sending this adorable, sweet baby to them. He brightened up even a bad day. She thought about how his dear little tongue didn't protrude very much at all and his cough was almost completely gone. Certainly he was a strong boy. Now, if these treatments could only help his mongolism, he might be normal and have a completely normal life.

"Edna Peak," the nurse's voice cut through Edna's thoughts. She picked up David and followed the nurse down the hall to the exam room.

"How are you today Mrs. Peak?" Doctor Stark asked as he walked in and greeted Edna with a warm smile. She liked Doctor Stark and thought he was one of the finest psychologists she had ever known, and she had known many.

"I've been alright, some good days, some bad. I'm glad to get my shots today." Edna giggled a little as she added, "Not everyone looks forward to getting a needle poked in their arm, but I do!"

Doctor Stark chuckled as he swabbed a small area on Edna's left arm with an alcohol-soaked cotton ball and then gave her the usual B12 shot - it seemed to help improve her overall mood and mentality. Then he asked about David. "Have you been giving him the hormone capsules I recommended last time you were here?"

"Yes, every day I give him half a capsule in his tomato juice."

"Very good. I want you to give him milk salts once a day along with the hormones and today I'd like to give David a shot of B12 as well. I think this may help him also."

Edna held David on her lap while Doctor stark swabbed his chubby thigh and then inserted the needle. David screamed and cried, and Edna kissed him and tried to sooth him. Once he had quieted, Doctor Stark reminded Edna, "I do believe that if you continue with the hormones and the shots, with time, David could be 100% normal."

"Oh, we are so hopeful, thanks to you, Doctor Stark!" Edna hugged David, kissed his tear-stained cheeks and continued, "Just the other day, Russell's mother remarked about the pretty shape of David's head. She said when Russell was a baby, the Governor of Utah, in whose house Russell was born, commented on the fine shape of Russell's head, and predicted that he would grow up into a manly man. Years later, he saw Mother Peak and Russell and reminded her of his prediction and that it had come true!"

"What a fine story Mrs. Peak. You have a good day and be sure to call me immediately if you have any real trouble." He smiled warmly at Edna and cooed at David for a moment and then walked them back to the waiting room.

Edna was anxious to get home and tell Russell what Doctor Stark had said. Maybe she would even surprise him at the store and bring him his favorite Fig Newton cookies.

*   *   *

Russell looked over Edna's shoulder at her fingers flying across the typewriter keys. Thank goodness he had bought her a strong, sturdy modern typewriter. She wrote page after page of journal entries. His eyes focused on the page as her thoughts came tumbling out into print:

Today David stood alone for about twenty seconds. He smiled the sassiest little smile – because he is so smart! Daddy was sitting on the bed laughing at him and I was kneeling to catch him when he toppled. He is so cute now! And his health is good, thanks to Heavenly Father. Dr. Stark is satisfied with him as he is improving right along. My heart is still sad at times when people comment on his eyes which droop when he is tired and his dear little mouth which he holds open with his tongue out a little at times. Otherwise he is so bright. He is very strong. I spent about ten minutes yesterday trying to put his diaper on!! He turned onto his stomach continually and giggled and peeked up at me so mischievously I laughed until I was weak.

Edna's hands paused as she stared at the typewriter, then slammed the return arm across the typewriter to begin a new paragraph.

Today has been an extremely hard strain emotionally.

Suddenly she jumped up out of her chair, almost clashing her head on Russell's chin. She turned around to face him and shouted, "Russell! You KNOW it strains my nerves when you read over my shoulder like that!" Her face was flushed with anger and her hands that were only moments ago so agile and nimble were clenched into tight fists at her side.

"I'm sorry darling. Please, do continue your writing. I won't look over your shoulder." Russell disappeared into the kitchen and returned a moment later with a cup of hot chocolate – one of Edna's favorite things. She looked up at Russell, smiled and graciously took a sip from the teacup.

Russell went into the adjoining living room and watched as David sat playing on the floor with his toys. It was amazing how easily entertained he was, a characteristic which was much appreciated by the whole family. With three very bright, very busy daughters, Edna would have a hard time with a colicky or difficult baby. "Where are Ginny, Deanna and Cherie?" Russell asked.

"They are planting flowers at the church building," replied Edna, without looking up from her typing.

Russell thought about all their good and faithful friends at church. He and Edna had decided to tell some of them about poor David's condition and they were all praying for him to improve and even to recover. It was June and David had been getting regular treatments for over 5 months. They thought they could see some improvement, but to have the faith of their friends and family was certainly comforting to them. One night, their good friend, Wynn Quist, came to the house to offer a special prayer for David. In it he said that David would, "Grow to manhood and would be a joy and comfort to his family." After the prayer was offered, Mr. Quist told them that, "They had nothing to worry about and that he had a very good feeling about David."

Russell thought about his own faith and how he believed in the power of God. His mind was swept back to when he was a boy, about twelve years old; he and his brother were crossing a field when Russell took hold of a low hanging wire. A live wire. His brother ran as fast as he could and found the place where the nearest switch was and shut the power off. Russell fell to the ground, limp. He said a prayer in his head for God to save him. The family doctor had said that Russell shouldn't be alive. His hand was so badly burned that Russell could reach in and touch the bone. But not only was he able to make use of the hand once again, there weren't even any noticeable scars.

Russell thought about how strong Edna's faith was too. She continued to believe that one day there would be something that would heal her mind. Russell hoped for this as well… maybe it would be so. Her doctor wasn't even positive about her diagnosis. "Probably schizophrenia" was what he had told her many years ago. At her worst times she underwent electric shock treatment – twice, sometimes three times in a week. Russell winced slightly just thinking about it, they sounded absolutely dreadful to him. But Edna was always willing, even anxious to undergo the treatments and said she felt better, at least for a time. The treatments did seem to help with her wild mood swings and depression. *Maybe something better will come along some day that will help her* he thought.

"RUSSELL!" Edna's shout finally broke through his thoughts. She had stopped typing and sat facing him. "Russell, I think I know what might have caused David's condition." She paused for a moment to make sure he was listening and not still lost in thought. "Remember when I was only a few months pregnant with him and I took Ginny and Deanna to the Crown Theatre? In the middle of the show a message from the management of the theatre flashed onto the screen that read: *There is a message for Mrs. Russell Peak at the manager's office."*

Russell looked blankly at Edna, wondering what in the world her story could possibly have anything to do with David's condition, but simply let her continue.

"When I got to the office, I was told to call home immediately. I called you and you told me that *CHERIE* was in the hospital! 'Come home quickly,' you had said. So then I RAN from the theater with the little girls behind me. I thought in my mind at the time, 'I don't care what happens to the baby, I've got to get to Cherie.' Of course when I arrived home I found out that it was your brother

JERRY not *CHERIE* who was in the hospital, but the shock to me and to the baby was done, as well as damage from me running all the way to the car."

Russell gave this some thought. Could it be possible? He didn't know. But he certainly didn't want Edna torturing her mind forever that *she* had caused David's mongolism. "I really don't think that would have damaged him, Edna. None of the doctor's we have ever taken him to have mentioned that it might have been caused by anything you could have done. All the same, it doesn't even matter how he came to be the way he is. He is a good boy. He is a good son." Russell patted David's head, and then added, "God made him just the way He wanted him."

With that said, Edna decided to voice something she had been thinking about for a while now, "I don't want David to have any more treatments. No more hormones, no more milk salts, no more shots. No more man-made anything. I just want to put our faith in God that if he wants David to be made whole, he will do it faster and better than any doctor could."

Russell stood and crossed the room to the table where Edna had placed her typewritten pages in a neat pile. He brushed his hand across the pages, thinking about what Edna was suggesting. Then, reaching for Edna's hand, he lifted her up, putting his arms around her and said, "That's a fine idea. I think you are right in this."

4

August 10, 1950

GINNY STOOPED DOWN and flipped the hot cakes over on the camping stove. She loved camping. The whole family did. Their daddy took the family camping a lot. He always told them, "Fresh air makes the mind clearer!" Now that she was twelve years old, she was beginning to understand what he meant by that. Yellowstone National Park was just the place to clear the mind.

"Breakfast is ready!" she hollered for everyone to come and eat. Russell was already knee-deep in the Madison River, fishing for trout. He was an expert fly fisherman and Ginny always loved to watch him fish. It was actually graceful; the way the rod floated back and forth, the line sweeping through the air and the tiny fly barely touching the water's surface. Whatever he caught that day they'd eat for lunch. Edna, 8-year-old Deanna and 7-year-old Cherie came to the picnic table and sat down.

"Where's Davie?" Edna asked the three girls as she glanced around their campsite. "Deanna, weren't you with him this morning?"

"Yes Mother, but then he went off looking for you. I thought you were just on the other side of the tent where he was going." Deanna's expression changed and her brow furrowed as she began to worry that she had done a poor job watching her little brother.

"I was down at the riverbank watching Daddy fish." The four of them began to get an uneasy feeling and immediately stood and began shouting, "DAAAAAAVID!" "DAAAAAVIE!" They searched the tent. They searched the car which was parked near the campsite. They searched down the trail towards the river and called and called his name. Nothing. Edna ran to get Russell who left the water quickly and breathlessly joined the others in the search. There was a growing panic amongst all of them.

He couldn't have gone far, he just barely learned how to walk Ginny thought as she peaked behind bushes and trees. He loved to give it a try but was not yet very profi-cient and still preferred crawling if he really wanted to get somewhere. With the ground still damp and so uneven and full of rocks, sticks, and other hazards for a crawling baby, it was unimaginable that he had in fact *crawled* off. If he were trying to walk, certainly he was still very nearby. The real problem was his talking. Even if he could hear their shouts for him, what would he do? Nothing. He had yet to say his first word. How would he answer back?

But they all shouted on. It helped with the nervous feeling they all had in their stomachs. Russell told the girls to go look for the baby near the road and he and Edna would look again toward the river. Heaven forbid he went to the river.

Within a few moments, on a trail that led to the road, Ginny found a toy David had been holding that morning. She shouted, "He's gone this way! Over here!" Russell, Edna, and the girls came running. They all walked quickly along the trail searching side to side trying to spot Davie and calling for him. Suddenly the brush cleared and opened up to the road. They looked to the right and there he was just a few yards away. He was sitting down cooing at something next to him. Ginny took a step toward him, then froze. Russell clamped his hand tightly around Ginny's mouth to keep her from screaming and Edna instinctively held the other two girls back on the trail. Ginny was horrified. David was sitting next to a snake. *He's going to get bit and die,* she thought. She shut her eyes as tight as she could, and her father whispered in her ear not to make a sound. She nodded her understanding and he slowly let go. As she stood trembling, her father gently coaxed David with his soothing voice, "Davie darling, come to Daddy. Leave the snake alone. Davie, please come to Daddy." David looked over his shoulder at Ginny and smiled. His soft, golden, curly hair caught the light just so and he looked cherubic. She wanted to run to him and snatch him up as quickly as she could, but she obeyed her father and stood still. She watched in utter amazement as David looked at the snake, cooed and babbled at it, then stood and took a shaky step toward them. He fell and Ginny couldn't help but let out a gasp.

Suddenly Ginny saw her father's arm whizz past her face, and his rod let out the line in a flash. Faster than Ginny could completely even understand what in the world her father was doing, the fishing line, with the fly attached to the end, coiled around the snake near its head probably at least a half dozen times, 'round and 'round, then Russell yanked back on the rod, ensnaring the snake instantly and lifting it off the ground and away from David. Ginny ran to Davie and snatched him up into her arms hugging and kissing him. Russell reeled the snake into the brush and disappeared momen-tarily. The girls heard a thud and squeezed their eyes shut tightly, not wanting to imagine the sight of the snake. Russell shouted out to them not to worry any more, the snake was dead.

Edna and the two little girls began to cry from their relief and the fright they had just experienced. Ginny stroked David's hair and felt the strength in her legs give way a little. For a moment she was angry at Deanna. *How could she let him out of her sight?* she thought. She looked at her poor mother who must be having fits by now. Her mother hated snakes even more than she did. Mother said they were all, "Devils on earth."

Edna was crying, but she wasn't scolding Deanna at all, she was hugging her! Ginny brought Davie to Edna who hugged him and squeezed him tightly and smothered him with her kisses. Davie giggled and basked in the attention, completely unaware of the drama that had just occurred or the danger he had been in.

As the family drove home the next day, Ginny leaned over the front seat and asked her father, "What kind of snake was that Daddy? Was it poisonous?"

"I believe it was a prairie rattlesnake, and yes, they are very poisonous."

Ginny's stomach felt sick about the whole thing all over again. She leaned back in her seat and looked out the window at the beautiful Wyoming scenery. *How could David sit right next to such a hideous creature? Why didn't the snake bite him?*

She knew why. David was special. Angels protected him.

5

December 1950

EDNA CAME RUSHING through the back alley door at Russell's shop, carrying two-year-old David on her hip. She seemed very excited about something and Russell's gaze fell to her form which was silhouetted by the light coming from the back door. Her green cotton dress flowed around her legs as she walked briskly toward Russell who couldn't help himself from admiring her great legs.

"Russell dear, I have something very interesting to tell you about!" she said as she placed David on the counter.

"So have I!" Russell said as he took her hand and led her to the back office/storage room. The room was quite messy; stacks of papers from the ground reached nearly two feet high, periodicals and books lay randomly about, and all sorts of his rod making supplies littered the small room. Russell knew how much it bothered Edna that he wouldn't let her organize it for him. But *he* knew where everything was, and the mess didn't bother *him*. He guided Edna through the mess to the back of the room and pointed to a picture that was sitting on his desk up against the wall. Edna stared at it.

Finally, she said, "Darling, why in heaven's name do you have a picture of Cinderella on your desk?"

"Remember the fellow I told you about that came into the store a few months ago – the fellow from Disney studios?" Edna nodded so Russell continued, "Well, he came in here today to see how his rod is coming – it's going to be a beauty Edna; I have done some really special things to it. I inset three tiny little rubies in the shape of Mickey Mouse! Anyway, he thought the rod was the most wonderful thing he ever saw. He liked it so much that he said he had something he wanted to give me. He went to his car and came back with this!" he said excitedly pointing to the picture. Edna stared at the picture, then back at Russell.

"And this is how he thanked you for a hand-made fishing rod with rubies inset into it? With a picture of Cinderella?" Edna was trying not to laugh.

"This one's special." Russell's blue eyes sparkled as he said, "Let me explain. The fellow's name is Kenneth Anderson, and he doesn't just *work* at Disney studios, he is the first assistant to Mr. Walt Disney himself! He is an artist and animator for Disney Pictures, and, by the way Edna, he wants to take our whole family on a tour of the studios – all we have to do is call him and arrange it!"

"Well, that does sound fun now, doesn't it" Edna interjected into Russell's story.

"Yes, it does. Anyway, this picture isn't a picture at all, it's called a 'cel' and it's an original Edna, it was used to make the motion picture. I think it's quite valuable." They both looked at the cel for a moment and then Russell added, "Not that I would ever sell it."

"That was very kind of him. I'll be sure to write him a note to thank him."

"The girls will have to write him too" Russell said as he reached down beside his desk and lifted up a fancy little pink bag. He reached inside and lifted out three little Mickey Mouse dolls with ribbons tied around their necks.

"My goodness Russell! The girls will be delighted!" Edna took one of the dolls and gazed at it, feeling the silkiness of the satin ribbon between her fingers.

Suddenly there was a crash of glass and Russell and Edna nearly jumped out of their skins and the Mickey Mouse doll in Edna's hand went flying nearly halfway across the room. David had knocked off a drinking glass that Russell had left on the edge of his desk and it had broken against the concrete floor. David began to wail, and Edna comforted him while Russell cleaned up the mess.

"I'm sorry dear," Edna said to Russell, "I completely forgot I was holding the baby and I didn't pay any attention to what his little hands were doing."

Russell scooped up the chunks of broken glass into a dustpan and said, "What's a silly glass?" He dumped the glass's remains into the garbage can and added, "He was just doing what a curious boy would do" and then kissed David on his tearstained cheek. "It's alright Davie, cheer up." Looking at Edna, Russell said, "So, sweetheart, you said you had something interesting to tell me about."

"Oh gracious, I almost forgot." Edna sat down at the desk and bounced David on her knees as she began her story. "I went to the Market Basket today and was in the produce department choosing fruits and vegetables when I noticed a tall, rather shabbily dressed elderly man. He stood in front of David's Taylor-Tot smiling benignly at him and I heard him say directly to David, 'You are a fine boy!' I thought nothing of it at first, but then, when I was standing at the check-stand, I saw him again and immediately was struck by the resemblance to my grandfather, Elisha Ledyard. He wore the same goatee as grandfather, was a little thinner than I remember him and had the same twinkle in his eye. I know I have never seen him at the market before and he didn't appear to be buying anything.

Russell, I believe it was actually my grandfather, sent here to comfort me and give me assurance that David will be alright." Edna paused for a moment, looking thoughtfully at David. "It has indeed given me new hope."

Russell was stunned. Was this her mind imagining things again? Why would her dead grandfather come back to a market to give her a message of hope? But then, even if it was her imagination or just simply an ordinary man she saw, if it gave her hope, maybe he shouldn't dismiss it.

He replied as quickly as he could figure out just what to say, "How extraordinary. You certainly should note this day in your journal dear." He reached out to David and took him up in his arms. David giggled in delight as he tapped his finger on Russell's glasses. Russell kissed his chubby cheeks and prodded him, "Say 'Dadda' Davie! Say 'Dadda'!" David just smiled and drooled, his tongue poking out of his mouth as it always did.

Edna began arranging papers and such on Russell's desk. "Do you believe me?" she sheepishly asked. Russell could tell that she now doubted her own account of the man at the grocery store. Oh boy, what should he answer? Immediately he had what he thought was a very clever idea.

"Uh oh. I think baby David has messed his diaper."

Edna stood quickly, took the baby from Russell, and started for the back door. "I'll see you at home darling, we'll have meatloaf for dinner tonight if you think you can come home early." She turned and kissed Russell. "The little girls will be so thrilled to see their daddy and hear of his new friend from Disney."

Russell watched from the front window as her car came from the alley and moved toward the light at the corner of Allen and Colorado Blvd. After her car disappeared around the corner he glanced at the edges of the window, admiring his clever work. Just the previous night, he and Edna had stayed up late decorating the store for Christmas. They had painted the front window to appear as if it was frosted over from a fresh snowfall. The affect was magical. He chuckled to himself to think what they had used to create the affect: a concoction they had borrowed from a neighbor. Quite funny really - stale beer and Epsom salts on Russ Peak's store window!

*   *   *

Christmas that year was dreamy for the whole family. The girls awoke at 3:30am and tried so hard to wake Edna and Russell. They were sent back to bed and fell asleep for a while. But by 5:00 they could stand it no longer and bounced and giggled on the bed until Edna and Russell agreed to get up.

The tree was decorated as it always was with strands of silver tinsel hanging from all of the branches. This year they had one problem with the tinsel though – David. He would take off all the strands he could reach and make a big pile of them on the living room floor. The tree would be stripped completely bare from about two feet down. It was the girls' job to put them back on, which they did, time after time. Edna had finally threatened to simply take all of the tinsel off for good that year and put it away in a box. But the three girls pleaded with her, "Mother, the tree simply won't look Christmassy without the tinsel!" So, the tinsel continued its almost daily journey from the tree to the floor, from the floor to the tree; on off, on off.

Virginia, Deanna, and Cherie ripped open their presents, squealing with delight. Their most favorite of all being a doll, about 15 inches high, with long brown hair they could style. She had a beautiful wooden closet with a bar for hanging clothes and a drawer for shoes and hats. Edna had spent the last four months hand sewing the doll a complete wardrobe. She had carefully bent wire to form tiny hangers for each item of clothing. Russell had painted the closet a lovely pale green color and Edna had carefully painted a bouquet of dainty flowers on the door. The three daughters spent all the rest of Christmas day dressing, undressing, and redressing the new doll.

David simply sat in the middle of the floor and rocked himself gently back and forth. He occasionally let out happy little squeals over the bright wrapping papers being strewn all over the living room floor. He was exceptionally pleased with a toy horn he had received from Santa, which he clutched tightly in his hands.

Edna and Russell were very proud of their daughters that year; the girls had saved their own money to purchase gifts for them: a silver necklace and a satin hose box for their mother, and a very nice belt with an initialed buckle, as well as a pair of suspenders for their father. The girls had also purchased a family favorite that year, a box of See's chocolates, which sat on the piano bench for everyone to help themselves to.

At the end of the day, Edna tucked David into bed and noticed he was still clutching his new toy horn. "David dear, put the horn down and go to sleep," she said as she kissed him goodnight.

"NO!"

Edna stared at him, her eyes wide. *How wonderful!* she thought. Up until this day, the only two things he had even tried to say was, "Dadda" – for Russell of course, and "Ed-dadda" when he wanted her. Now he had said a real word, clear as day.

"David, you really shouldn't say that to your mother" she said, remembering to correct his misbehavior.

"NO!" he shouted at her, and then gave her a mischievous smile.

Edna turned on her heal and swiftly walked out of the room before the mischievous little gentleman could see her smile and the happiness in her eyes.

6

July 4, 1951

HAPPY BIRTHDAY!" EVERYONE whooped as they entered Edna's hospital room carrying balloons, gifts, and Edna's favorite chocolate cake. They had all come - Russell, Ginny, Deanna, Cherie, David, Edna's father, and both of Russell's parents. It was a lousy way to spend a birthday, not to mention Independence Day, so they were trying to make it festive and cheery any way.

Ginny looked at her mother who didn't look happy at all. She looked despondent. Edna hardly seemed to notice the commotion when they all entered. Every year the Fourth of July was the grandest day of the year for Mother, but at that moment Ginny wondered if her mother had forgotten it was her own birthday. Ginny began to feel upset and looked at her father for some kind of reassurance. Russell put a hand on Ginny's shoulder and squeezed it gently.

"Edna darling, your dad is here, and the girls, and David" Russell said. "We're all here for your birthday. Won't you sit up a bit and have some of your favorite chocolate cake – Virginia and Deanna made it for you." He went to Edna's bedside and stroked her hair, adding, "And of course it's Cherie's birthday tomorrow. She'll be eight, and this way you can wish her a happy birthday too."

Edna looked up at him and then at the girls and David. She managed to smile a weak smile at Cherie and whispered, "Happy birthday Dear." Then, turning to her father said, "Thank you. Why don't you all go home now." She put her head back on the pillow and stared at the wall.

"Edna, don't you want to open your presents?" her father asked, and held up a package wrapped in red paper with an oversized silver bow.

She didn't look at him.

*   *   *

Two nights earlier, Ginny had volunteered to prepare dinner and was in the kitchen, frying chicken. Edna was helping her by making gravy, when she moaned in pain and dug her fingers into her side. Ginny turned from the chicken and asked if she was alright.

"No dear, go call your father."

Ginny was frightened. Was her mother going to die? She quickly called the store and rushed through the words, "Daddy, come home right now, Mother is...Mother said...something's wrong and you need to come home right now." She hung up before waiting for her father to reply and rushed back into the kitchen to find Edna stooped over the stove, still holding her side and with a very strained look on her face.

"Mother, please go lie down on the couch. Daddy will be home in just a few minutes."

"Thank you dear. What would we ever do without you, Virginia?" She put her arm around Ginny's shoulder for support, and Ginny, who was thirteen years old and almost as tall as Edna now, helped her slowly walk into the living room and then gently helped her get somewhat comfortable on the couch.

By now the other two girls noticed their mother's distress and stood frozen in the middle of the living room, staring at Edna.

"Are you gonna die, Mother?" Cherie asked.

Edna managed to giggle slightly and said, "No darling. I'm not going to die. Be a good girl and entertain David in his bedroom for a little while."

Cherie took David's hand and led him to his room. Ginny looked at her mother and asked if she could get her anything.

Just then, her father's car pulled into the driveway and Russell came running through the front door. "Edna! What's wrong?"

"I'm not exactly sure, I think it may be an appendicitis attack."

"Ginny, take care of the children, I'm taking Mother to the hospital," Russell said as he assisted Edna in standing up from the couch. He helped her out to the car and Ginny watched as they drove out of sight. *What's an appendicitis attack?* She wondered, letting her imagination go wild. She had overheard her daddy once telling a friend that he was always afraid that Edna could have a complete breakdown someday. Was this it? *Will Mother ever come home again? She seemed herself, except, of course, for the pain in her side. Is an "appendicitis attack" the same thing as a "complete breakdown?"* Ginny's eyes welled up and she quickly turned to check on the others, hoping it would keep her from crying. She couldn't help but let a few tears fall in spite of her efforts, but wiped them away before Deanna or Cherie, or especially David, could see them. David would be particularly upset to see her crying.

Now, two days later, Ginny was once again wondering if her mother was going to be alright. Her father had explained what an appendicitis was and that her mother would be just fine because she had had an operation to remove the ailing organ. He said she would be "as good as new." But she didn't seem fine or good as new. Something was wrong.

*   *   *

Edna was in the hospital for one week recovering. When she came home, she seemed herself again, only a little tired and sore. Ginny had managed most of the time to do the basic necessities – cooking and keeping the house tidy. Grandpa Ledyard had also helped tremendously. He would come over every day and play with David and do laundry so that Edna wouldn't be troubled by it upon her return. Russell had been at the store his usual late hours, but every morning he would go to the hospital and visit Edna. He always told the girls the same report, "Mother is going to be just fine."

Not an hour after her return home, there was a knock on the front door. It was Mr. Summerhays from church, a very dear friend and leader of their congregation. "How are you feeling, Edna?" he asked as he took a seat in the chair facing Edna, who was resting on the couch.

"Oh, much better now. I'm so glad to be home and out of the hospital."

"I hope I'm not disrupting your homecoming."

"Of course not. You're a most welcome visitor." Edna reached over to the end table for a box of See's candy and held them out to Mr. Summerhays. "Please have a chocolate," she said with her usual cheery smile.

Taking one and popping it into his mouth he said, "Barbara and I ran across a book that we thought you might enjoy. We know how much you read," he said, motioning to the piles of books that were on the end tables, books in the bookshelves next to the fireplace, and books stacked on top of the piano. As he handed her the book he had brought, he added, "It's by the minister Harry Emerson Fosdick, and it's entitled *The Meaning of Faith*. I thought chapter 6 would be of particular interest to you – it's called, *Faith's Greatest Obstacle.*"

Edna thumbed through the book for a moment, turning to chapter 6.

Mr. Summerhays continued, "I've given a lot of thought to your situation with David's condition, and I have come to feel that there are three things I would like you to remember. First, God has not sent this affliction to you because of any sin you have committed. Second, the condition was not inflicted upon David because his spirit is a handicapped spirit. His spirit is perfect. And third, always remember to pray that God will grant you the strength, courage, and fortitude to accept God's will and to ask Him, if it is His will, that David may be made whole." He looked at Edna with compassion, hoping that he did not, in any way, offend.

"You are so very kind. Thank you ever so much for your thoughtfulness and words of encouragement and council." Edna held the book up in front of her and said, "I look forward to reading the book!"

He stayed a short while and visited about the other family members and their summer activities. Edna enjoyed the visit entirely and was left with an abiding faith in God and His ways and a bright hope for the future. She began reading the book immediately after Mr. Summerhays left and had read through nearly half the book by the time Russell returned home from work that evening.

"Russell dear, Mr. Summerhays visited today and gave me a most wonderful book! Come here, I want to read something to you." Russell walked over to the couch, bent down and kissed Edna's forehead, then sat in his favorite comfortable chair. He reached for the box of chocolates but was disappointed to find them all gone.

"In the sixth chapter, titled *Faith's Greatest Obstacle*, the author, who is a minister, says, 'The basis of any intelligent explanation of faith's problem must rest in a right practical attitude toward trouble.' Don't you find that interesting?" She continued, "I think we would do well to change our attitude towards David's troubles."

Russell shifted slightly in his chair and asked, "What do you mean exactly?"

"Well, I guess I speak for myself when I say that I have been a little demanding in my prayers for David. I have wanted him to be made whole *now.* I think I must finally submit to God's will for David and trust that someday, maybe only when he is in Heaven, will he be made whole."

"Are you saying we should give up?" Russell asked incredulously.

"Not give up! More like...*give in.*"

"*Give in?*"

"Yes. Give in to God's will. Instead of ours."

Russell had to think for a moment. Edna sat and patiently let him mull it over in his mind. She knew she had been reading and thinking about this nearly half the day, and now she was suddenly asking Russell to change his thinking too.

Russell sat silently thinking for what seemed to Edna to be a very long time. But she sat quietly and let him think. She had learned a long time ago that Russell was a very thoughtful man and usually didn't rush to any conclusions about anything. Finally, he spoke, "There really isn't much fault you can find in what you just said, is there? God's will is always right. I do have faith in Him and He knows what's best for our family – for you and for me. It's just hard to accept that maybe His will is different than what I, we, really want for our son." Russell was thoughtful again for a moment, then continued, "Maybe there are things for us to learn through David's troubles that we wouldn't learn otherwise. We can't always know God's purposes in everything. Can we?"

7

August 13, 1951

EDNA SAT ON the front porch, watching the children play in the front yard. Russell had spent the morning repairing the sink drain in the bathroom and was finally backing out of the driveway to leave for work. As soon as he turned her way, she blew a kiss to him. Russell suddenly stopped the car, got out and came to her. Bending over, he took her face in his hands, kissed her, and said, "I forgot to kiss my sweetheart goodbye." Edna smiled up at him, so thoroughly happy to be married to him. Russell turned and walked back to his car, saying goodbye to the children and smiling as they giggled and shouted out their goodbyes to him in return.

Edna watched his car until it was out of sight, then tore open the envelope from the letter she had received in the mail that morning. It was a letter from Paul, her older brother, and she was anxious to hear news from him, hoping he was feeling better.

My Darling Sister, Edna,
How very compassionate and kind to your brother you are!

I am deeply grateful to you for your visit two weeks ago. I know you must have been still a little tired from your own ordeal with your appendicitis attack, and yet you came such a considerable distance to be with me in my time of great need. How I love you for it. Just to hear your giggle and listen to your funny stories of the children lifted my spirits more than you can imagine.

I want to especially thank you for loaning me your book on faith by Mr. Fosdick. I enjoyed it immensely and learned a great deal. I have never been religious like you, but I do have a general belief in God that is now stronger, thanks to you, dear sister, and to Mr. Fosdick.

I must tell you of something that I think you should know. When I first became ill and was brought here, to the sanitarium, I thought of ending my life. I didn't feel I could go on any longer, so deep was my despair. I didn't understand God, or why he had afflicted my mind. I don't profess any great understanding now, but I do, however, seem to have enough understanding as to give me hope for the future and a new resolve to continue on in my life's challenges.

The following are my favorite quotes from the book, which I intend to memorize so as to have them in my head, ready for the moment when I may need to use them.

"Noble characters do not alone bear trouble, they use it!"

"Nothing, save adversity can ever build patience, courage, sympathy and power."

"Character grows on trouble."

"Trouble develops and reveals character."

I know you have struggled with the same affliction as I, and that you and Russell have been given a challenge with David's condition. I see how this fine book has helped you as well, and I am glad for it.

In closing, I wish to thank you most sincerely for the little bookmark you made and inserted into the book which read:

"Whom the Lord loveth, He chasteneth. Hebrews 12:6"

As I said, I don't understand everything, but I do feel loved, which sometimes I am able to find humor in when connected to the scripture on the bookmark! Please give Russell my best regards, and hugs and kisses to my nieces and nephew from their Uncle Paul.

Your loving and devoted brother,
Paul
P.S. I will be going home next Tuesday!

Edna wiped the tears from her face and looked up at the sunny California sky. She felt oddly sad and happy at the same moment. Her heart ached for Paul when he suffered with his depression so severely. She looked at the girls and David playing happily on the front lawn. *Such blessings,* she thought.

"Children, we all must end our fun now and go inside."

The girls moaned in protest, but their feet began to move toward the porch.

"I know you were having such fun, but we have to pack for our vacation. We leave tomorrow!"

The girls squealed in delight at the thought of the family

camping trip and rushed happily inside to pack and get everything ready.

Edna added, "And your Uncle Paul sends his love to you all."

The girls asked Edna if they were going to be able to see him soon, for they adored their Uncle Paul.

8

August 14 – 30, 1951

BAKER'S HOLE WAS one of the family's favorite places to
camp. This year was going to be particularly fun because
Ken Anderson, from Disney studios, his wife Polly, and their
three daughters, and even Mrs. Anderson, Ken's mother, had all
come along too. Ken was an excited fly fishing "student" of Russell's,
and there was no place like West Yellowstone to get an education.

The entire first week was glorious. The weather was perfect, and
Ken and Russ fished every day for hours. Russ showed him which
flies to use and how to cast properly. He also showed him a few good
casting tricks. "Watch this one," Russ said, then quickly swung his
right arm out wide, then whipped his fishing rod behind his back.
In an instant, he gave the grip a tight flick, causing the reel to spin
and the line to go flying out to the water.

"Hah! That was amazing!" Ken's eyes were wide with wonder
and excitement. "I heard you could cast behind your back, but I
didn't believe it! Teach me to do that!"

Russ gave him some instruction and Ken tried. Ken Failed.
But the two had a few good laughs in the process.

Standing in the water up to their thighs, they would sometimes fish for long periods of time without saying one word. The air was so fresh and the water so clean. They would get lost in their own thoughts to the rhythm of their rods stroking back and forth, back and forth. Every little while their quiet thoughts were broken by the sound of one of them hollering, "I got one!" Each catch was surveyed for size, color, and species. They kept the best ones for dinner and gently lowered the rest back into the water and watched them swim away.

When they did talk, they mostly talked shop. Ken wanted to know how in the world Russ made fishing rods and Russ wanted to know how in world Ken made movies. Two men, from two very different worlds, but good friends. Then Ken asked a question which startled Russell a bit, "What's wrong with your son, David?"

Russell wasn't sure how to answer at first. No one had ever really dared to be so bold. "He's a mongoloid," he answered matter-of-factly.

"What exactly is that?"

"Actually, we don't really know. The doctors don't know much about it, like what causes it or how to treat it. They just know that mongoloids all have similar facial features and characteristics. And they have limited intelligence." The facts made up such a short list. All he could explain were the facts.

"Is he going to go to school?" Ken asked.

Russell had never even thought about this. He had gotten so caught up in hoping David could get better that he had never considered school. "I don't know," he answered honestly. Then added, "I surely would hope so! But I suppose he might not be able to."

"I once knew a child who looked like David, the same kind of eyes and all, but she had heart problems and she died before she was three years old."

"Gee whiz Ken. Thanks for the great story, but David seems to be healthy as a horse."

Ken quipped back, "I once knew a horse who had heart problems and fell to the ground dead as a doorknob one day."

Ken knew just how to get Russell to lighten up and laugh about something. It wasn't that he was trying to be insensitive, he simply knew that one must laugh at life sometimes. And laugh they did. Russell felt relief from it and knew he was too serious and private about David and his condition. Ken brought humor to almost everything – perhaps that's why Russell enjoyed his company so much. Life felt almost perfect at that moment: fishing in a stream, fresh air, the smell of pine, crystal clear water, family, and good friends.

$$* \quad * \quad *$$

The rain came down in torrents. Then it became sleet. Then hail. Then…Snow! How could it be *snowing* in August? The two families stayed in their tents, hoping the weather would miraculously clear up.

"Rain, rain, go away! Come again some other day!" the children chanted over and over.

"Girls, ENOUGH!" Edna's nerves were frazzled. She put her hand on baby David's forehead for the hundredth time that day. Still hot. "Deanna, hand me the spoon and the jam darling, and I'm sorry I shouted at you girls."

Deanna handed Edna the spoon and jam and said, "We're sorry Mother, we can be quiet for you."

"You are always such good girls, what would I do without you." Edna smiled at Deanna and then took an aspirin and crushed it up and added jam. She then tried to coax David into opening his mouth, but David was being stubborn about it. He flung his arm at the spoon, sending the spoon flying across the tent, splatting on the wall, and finally coming to rest on Ginny's cotton flannel sleeping bag.

"Davie dear, you simply *must* eat the jam. And it's delicious! It will help your teeth feel better." Edna pried open his mouth and touched his gums where two teeth were trying mightily to burst their way into David's mouth. David began to wail in pain again. Edna began the process all over again: spoon, jam, aspirin. This time she enlisted the help of the girls who all stood behind her and made silly faces until David laughed, then she quickly stuck the spoon in his mouth, took his chin in her hand and forced him to shut his lips around the spoon. It worked! Edna smiled at him. Unexpectedly David opened his mouth and spit all the red jam out onto Edna's blouse.

Edna was about to cry in frustration when the girls all burst into laughter. "I guess it *is* funny. A little," she said, trying to convince herself. "OK girls. One more try. This time I won't take my hand off his mouth until we hear him swallow."

Spoon, jam, aspirin, silly faces, laugh, insert spoon, hold chin. Hold chin. Hold chin. "Come on Davie, don't be stubborn. Swallow."

The girls began to chant, "Swallow, swallow, swallow!"

David swallowed.

"Hurray! Hurray for David!" The girls danced a little jig and Edna breathed a sigh of relief, picked up David and held him while he whimpered in defeat.

Our misery should be all over with just as soon as these two teeth break through, Edna thought to herself. And the weather was bound to clear up.

Certainly, things couldn't get worse.

✳   ✳   ✳

The entire next week was spent by the two families enduring the stomach flu which passed through everyone like falling dominoes. Russell worried about Edna's mood and thought it best to head for home as soon as everyone was well enough to begin the two-day drive.

They said their farewells to the Andersons, who were tired and weak, but managed to smile and say what a grand time they had had. "Now we can say our friendship has endured hail!" Ken said, grinning. They all laughed until they sputtered and held their weakened tummies in their hands. The two men shook hands, the wives hugged one another, and the girls gave each other small tokens of their new friendship: special rocks they had found in the river. The two families waved furiously to each other as the Peak's car drove out of the campsite.

Russell drove most of the time, but Edna took over so he could rest a bit and did the driving through Nevada. She was dismayed at how uninteresting and boring the scenery was and drove a little bit too fast.

"Russell dear, wake up." Edna had pulled over and was trying to stir Russell who had fallen asleep. "I'm very sorry to have to tell you this, but, chump that I am, I drove 60 miles per hour through wet oil. If there was a sign, I didn't see it."

Russell silently got out and surveyed the damage. The car and trailer were covered with black, sticky oil. He sighed and simply said, "I suppose we'll have to scrub it off before we go much further. How far from the next town are we?"

"I think about 10 miles."

"If you see any more oil, Edna, slow down." Russell winked at her so that she knew he was not angry with her. What was the point of being angry with her? The damage to the car was done. Why damage her feelings as well?

It took almost one and a half hours for Russell to get all the oil scrubbed off with benzine which he had purchased at a small local auto shop. Once on their way again, Russell asked, "Did you have any fun at all dear?"

"Oh yes, I most certainly did! You know I love to camp. Even with all the trials, I would jump at the chance to go again."

Russell was surprised. He thought for sure she would be depressed about the trip. Things had gone so poorly. "I love you," he said, looking over at Edna and taking her hand that was resting in her lap.

"I love you too. Thank you for not being sore at me about the oil. You are the dearest husband!"

9

December 26, 1951

EDNA, HER FATHER, Virginia, and Edna's Aunt Inez, sat with anticipation, not moving their eyes from the closed curtains. The amphitheater was full to capacity, and there was a hush as the grey velvet draperies slowly and soundlessly began to draw to the sides. The faint sound of Handle's *Messiah* could be heard over the loudspeakers that flanked the stage.

As the curtains pulled back, the center of the famous painting was revealed. Christ, with a scarlet robe on the ground behind him and the cross that was to be his lying on the ground at his feet, stood and gazed heavenward. The two thieves stood bound, a short distance behind Him. The curtains pulled back farther to reveal Mary the mother of Jesus, supported on both sides by John the Beloved and another disciple, and others of Christ's followers standing with them. Next to them was the weeping Mary Magdalene, kneeling on the ground in solitude, a distraught figure in a white dress, alone, forlorn, with her face in her hands. The curtains, almost completely drawn open, revealed the Roman soldiers, Caiaphas, and the arrogant

High Priests on the other side. The curtains finally came to a rest, leaving the painting completely exposed. To the far right, in the distance, was the walled city of Jerusalem where Christ had received his fateful judgement. The sky was dark, foreboding, and looming over the crowds of people, with the exception of a stream of faint light, coming from the heavens and resting on Jesus.

It was magnificent. Inspiring. Overwhelming. The four of them sat silently with the hundreds of others in the theatre as they stared at the mammoth painting. It was 195 feet long and 45 feet high. The theatre, at Forest Lawn in Glendale, was custom built just to accommodate the masterpiece entitled, "The Crucifixion" by the polish painter Jan Styka. It was the largest religious painting in the world and had finally found a permanent home in California, just miles from Pasadena, and Edna especially had badly wanted to see it.

Edna wiped her cheeks with a dainty linen hankie she kept in her purse. She tried to stop crying but couldn't. She wiped tears until the hankie was without dry spots. Noticing her distress, her father put a gentle hand on her shoulder and asked her if she would like to leave. She smiled, grateful for his tenderness, but whispered, "Thank you Daddy, but no, I'm fine. I would very much like to stay."

She returned her attention to the painting. She wanted to emblazon it in her mind. She stared and stared until she felt she could describe it in detail, the figures, the colors, the emotion. She closed her eyes and pictured it in her head.

People began to leave after a while, but Edna sat sill. Her father, her aunt and her daughter stayed with her. They sat and waited while Edna stared at the painting.

Finally, Edna stood and wistfully said, 'Why don't we go home now."

10

December 30, 1951

RUSSELL SAT IN the chair listening to Edna. He couldn't believe it. Certainly she was, at the very least, letting her imagination get away with her. She had been shopping at the Market Basket again, to get a pot roast for their Sunday dinner. She thought she saw something peculiar. Maybe he should suggest that she shop somewhere else. That might do the trick. No, probably it wouldn't.

"As I entered the store, I immediately saw a woman who was dressed very oddly," Edna had begun. "She seemed to be quite old. She wore a long black coat down to almost covering her shoes and she had a scarf over her head. I wondered if she was another angel! I looked at her back, which she had turned toward me and at her shoes, which were black and worn grey at the heel. She had looked right at me when I entered the store and then turned quickly and, I thought, put some change into her purse if she had one, I couldn't see. Then she hastened out of the store." Edna took a deep breath and continued her story, "As I shopped for the pot roast I pondered on the strangeness of the woman. Her face struck me as quite beautiful for someone so old and I wondered if she was perhaps one of my relatives."

Not another dead relative, Russell thought, and smiled inside despite his genuine concern.

"I found a lovely roast for only 81 cents a pound, which was such a remarkable bargain I at once thought she had caused the reasonable price. Upon coming home, I told the girls that I had seen an angel! They were as impressed with the story as I." Edna paused and looked at Russell who was staring at her, his brow slightly furrowed in concern. He sat motionless, silent.

Edna looked down at David who was sitting on the floor playing with a stack of blocks. She gazed about the room, searching her mind for other possible insights. "I suppose it strange that an angel would be wearing black..." her voice trailed off while she fell into deep thought. Russell was still flabbergasted into silence. Edna kept thinking, fiddling with her car keys absentmindedly. "Maybe she was an evil spirit... maybe she had some evil intent and hurried out of the store when she saw me because she could see all around me my guardian angels, which, of course, I could not see." Edna looked at Russell again, hoping this possible explanation would make more sense. He simply sat still, speechless, staring at her. "Yes. Yes, the more I think about it, Russell, the more I think this was the case."

*   *   *

Russell stared out the window at the stars. It was a full moon and a very bright night. But the moon was not the thing that was keeping him awake. He glanced over at Edna, sleeping soundly. Her brown, wavy hair had fallen across her face slightly and Russell reached over and gently brushed it back. She looked so pretty in the moonlight. He watched her sleep, her breaths barely even noticeable. He gently touched the pink silk nightgown covering her shoulder. So lovely. He kissed her cheek and whispered, "I love you." He knew she couldn't hear him, but he had to say what he felt.

He thought about the remarkable story she had related to him earlier that day. *How could someone so smart have such difficulty deciphering between real and imagined* he wondered. He never could understand how her brain worked, or in this case, *didn't* work. Russell lay on his back and looked once again out the window at the stars. His poor, darling Edna. He wished so badly that her mind wouldn't do these things to her. As long as he'd known her, she had struggled with these problems.

He had fallen in love with her so easily. It felt completely natural, like sitting down in a comfortable chair that you've sat in for years. But a few months after he began courting her, she ended up in the sanitarium. He couldn't see her for weeks. Nevertheless, he stopped by every day after work to check on her. The nurses all knew him by name and would give him what small bits of information they could.

Her doctor had spoken to him one day as he waited in the lobby, hoping to be allowed to see Edna.

"So, you're the young man who's been coming to see Miss Ledyard?"

"Yes, that's right," Russell answered, shyly digging his hands deep into his pants' pockets.

"You know, she most likely won't spend more than a few years of her whole life outside of an institution." The doctor casually put a cigarette to his lips and lit it while Russell searched his mind for how to reply.

"Oh, that may not be true. Poor kid is just having a hard time of things. You know, life has been hard for her, with her mother dying and her having to take care of her brothers and father, and work and go to school. She just needs some extra rest." Russell was half trying to convince himself as well.

"Son, I've been treating Edna for years now. It's a lot more than needing some rest. She'll just get worse and worse until there comes a day when she'll never leave the sanitarium. You'd be really smart to go home and try to forget her. Find someone who's normal."

Russell's blue eyes glazed over as he stared hard at Edna's doctor. The thought of never seeing Edna again was a bitter pill, one he refused to swallow.

"Thank you for taking such good care of her," he finally said as he offered his hand to shake.

Russell returned the next day. And the next and the next. When he was finally permitted to see her, he told her he loved her. Every day he visited Edna. He read to her, wrote her notes, and brought her favorite chocolates. Little by little, she recovered.

Russell had felt tormented over the situation. How was such a simple man going to take care of such a complex woman? He'd find a way. He had to. He couldn't live without her. At least, he didn't ever *want* to live without her.

Russell's eyelids felt heavy as he rolled onto his side and put his arm around Edna's waist. She squirmed a tiny bit and sleepily whispered, "I love you." His mind began to drift off, the moonlight faded... Russell fell asleep.

II

February 22, 1952

GINNY COULDN'T BELIEVE her ears! Could it be true? She looked out the window at the beauty of the canyon as she, Mother, Deanna, Cherie and David drove over to Glendale by way of Bouquet Canyon. Her mother was crying now.

"I know I am not the ideal wife. I'm sure he has run across someone who *is* his ideal and he has tried bravely to conceal it from me. He is martyr-like trying to make the best of a sad and hopeless situation and is simply pitying me. He doesn't love me anymore." Edna pulled the car over into a state park parking lot and dabbed at her tears. Ginny sat silent, thinking. The other two girls had been chattering in the back seat, only half listening, but were now concerned over their mother's sobbing.

"Daddy did say something unusual the other day at church, Mother," Ginny began to remember. "He said that there was something that would shock the congregation if he mentioned it." Edna's eyes grew wide and she let out new sobs. Three-year-old David began to mock-cry at the sight of Edna's crying, copying her. He always copied their emotions; cried when someone cried or laughed when someone laughed, and the family didn't know if it was because he thought that's would he should do, or if he truly felt the same emotions. Ginny reached over and comforted him.

Trying to bravely pull herself together, Edna told the children to get out of the car and go explore the canyon stream. They forgot the drama in the car for a short while as they all played in the stream, collected rock specimens and ate a picnic lunch together.

"Girls, we better get going, I'm not feeling too well." Edna gathered up David and the girls cleaned up the mess from the picnic. Once back in the car, David fell asleep stretched out on the front seat, with his head in Edna's lap and his feet on Ginny's.

*　　*　　*

"Edna! How could you possibly think such a thing?" Russell's face was flushed. "And you expressed it to the girls too!" He shook his head in utter disbelief. "I am completely mystified by your behavior. Why don't you trust me?" Russell was actually angry. He almost never got angry and when he did, it was for good reason.

Edna recounted what had led up to her suspicions. When she told of what Ginny had heard him say to someone at church Russell began to laugh. He laughed harder but choked out the words, "Oh Edna, you can't be serious?" He looked at her with a grin and asked, "Would you like to know what I was referring to?"

Edna, flushed and embarrassed, nodded her head.

"I was referring to the trouble I am having with the boys and girls in my Sunday School class. And the preacher's son is the worst of the bunch!"

Edna felt ashamed. Russell gently pulled her to him and said, "I only love *you*. I will love you forever, no matter what. You *are* the ideal wife *for me*."

"Oh Russell, my darling Russell, please forgive me," Edna sobbed with deep, heartfelt humility.

"You're forgiven," he said, wiping her tears as they fell with the handkerchief he drew from his pant's pocket. He simply held her and let her cry. He told himself that it was probably a bad case of Edna's paranoia doing mean tricks on her mind. She didn't really mistrust him.

Edna's tears soaked through Russell's cotton work shirt and she finally was able to feel better and peaceful. Thank heaven he had such a forgiving nature. But relieved as she was, she still felt sick in her stomach for some reason.

12

February 26, 1952

"Mrs. Peak."

Edna rose from her seat in the waiting room and followed the nurse down the hall. She waited only a few moments before Dr. Robinson appeared. "How are you today Mrs. Peak?" He had been their family doctor for the past 15 years and knew the family well.

"I'm here because I am a little concerned over some unusual bleeding... and I haven't been feeling well in general." It was difficult to talk to a man about rather personal female issues, even if he was a doctor.

Dr. Robinson thought for a few moments, looking at her record file. "I'd like to perform a "Q test" on you.

"A Q test, my goodness. Are you sure that's the test I need? And I've heard of it, but isn't it a rather new test? Are the results accurate?"

"Yes, it has proved itself to be very accurate and as a matter-of-fact you will be the first person I have used this test method on," he said, motioning for his nurse to fetch the needed supplies.

"My, don't I feel special!" Edna said with a giggle.

He asked for her left arm, which she placed across the table then inserted a needle to inject the testing fluid. Unfortunately, he put the needle in a bit too far, injecting the fluid incorrectly, making the test void. So, he asked for her right arm.

"I'm beginning to wish I was your hundredth person instead of your first!" Edna laughed.

"I apologize, Mrs. Peak, the distinction of being the first isn't worth it, huh?" He had prepared her right arm and was now slowly, carefully, inserting the needle once again.

"Perfect," he announced. "Based on your reaction, we should know in about 30 minutes what the result is."

Edna took advantage of the 30 minutes to run across the street and have a quick lunch. She sat at a booth, working the crossword puzzle in the newspaper to keep her mind off the test.

Once back in Dr. Robinson's office, she felt a bit nervous. He looked at her arm for only a moment, then at her.

Mrs. Peak, congratulation! You are positively pregnant!"

*   *   *

Edna burst into the store through the back door.

"Russell, I have something to tell you!" Edna was almost out of breath with excitement.

Not another Market Basket sighting I hope, Russell thought. He turned from his lathe to find Edna grinning at him.

"Another little Peak is on the assembly line!" she burst out.

Russell stared at her. Disbelief written all over his face. "Are you certain?"

"Yes, quite. I went to Dr. Robinson's this afternoon and he did a new test called a "Q test" which is supposedly more accurate than the previous types of pregnancy tests. He said I was positively PG!"

Russell still stood staring, dumbfounded. His mind couldn't help but immediately think about the possibility of another boy. A normal boy. Finally, he was able to speak, "Why that's just swell, Darling. Are you feeling alright?"

"Well, I feel excited right now, of course, but I've felt a little nauseated lately and… well, this explains it doesn't it." She planted an excited kiss on Russell's cheek and as she began to walk toward the back door added, "Dr. Robinson told me I must stay in bed until I quit spotting, so I better go, but I just *had* to come by first and tell you."

Russell walked her out to the car and told her again how excited he was. As she drove out of the parking lot he felt a little anxious. She had been so up and down lately. Maybe the pregnancy was the explanation for that as well. He hoped so.

*   *   *

"Hand me that chart dear." Edna pointed to a large genealogy chart lying on the floor. Deanna picked it up and handed it to her mother who had been laid up in bed for almost a full week now.

"What are all these charts for anyway, Mother?"

"They are genealogy charts I use to record our ancestors. My parents, their parents, their parents' parents and so forth." Edna held up a poster sized chart with a giant tree printed as background. Tiny names were carefully printed in Edna's handwriting all over the sprawling branches of the tree.

Deanna looked closely at the names on the tree and began reading them out loud. "Edna Gertrude Ledyard. That's you Mother! Gurdon Hoyt Ledyard, Gertrude Lena Barclay. Isn't that grandpa and grandmother?" Deanna asked.

"Yes dear," Edna answered absentmindedly as she searched the chart for a name she was looking for.

Deanna continued reading the names, "Elisha Gurdon Ledyard, Ida Maria Hoyt," Deanna took a deep breath. "We have a lot of relatives, don't we mother?"

Edna laughed, "We sure do, darling. Isn't it wonderful?"

"Do you like doing these charts more than reading?" Deanna motioned to the stack of books on the nightstand.

"Oh, I don't know. That's a tough question," Edna sighed. "I suppose I like them both about the same."

Deanna poked around quietly for a while then left the room to play. Edna returned to her charts. There were papers, charts, books, family journals, birth records, death records, and marriage records strewn all over the bed and floor. Edna had a passion for it, just like reading. Every night when Russell finally came home from the store, he would have to clear all of it off the bed before he could even see the sheets. At least it seemed to keep her mind busy. And happy.

13

April 20, 1952

YOU STAY AT the store late to avoid me!" Edna accused Russell. "You hate being at home, don't you? DON'T YOU?" she screamed at him. She had been in a tirade for nearly an hour now. "You love that darn store more than you love your own family!" Edna grabbed the nearest item she could find, one of Russell's small tackle boxes and threw it in the water.

Russell had brought her out on a rented boat at Lake Henshaw. He knew she had been feeling very poorly and thought that perhaps a day trip to one of her favorite spots would help. Right now, he was feeling quite mistaken. "Edna, darling, why don't you calm down and sit by me for a moment."

"CALM DOWN?" This suggestion seemed to enrage Edna more. "CALM DOWN? How can I calm down with a husband who wishes I were dead?" She began to sob uncontrollably. "*I wish I were dead!*" she shrieked. Edna plunked down in the boat seat and lifted her knees up to her face, wrapped her arms around her bent legs, hid her face into her arms and cried.

"Oh Edna, you don't mean that. We have a baby coming. Sweetheart… please. Look at me." Edna refused to lift her face from her arms and continued to cry. "What a wonderful thing – aren't you happy – "

"DO I SEEM HAPPY TO YOU RUSSELL?" she interrupted and jumped up from her position in the seat to stand over him.

Russell stood and tried to hold her, but she swung her arm up and over her shoulder to refuse the affection. "My doctor told you not to marry me. So why did you? Huh? WHY Russell? Why would you marry a crazy like me?" She was still sobbing and flung herself to the other side of the boat.

"I married you because I loved you. Please, Edna, please believe me. I love you darling."

"DON'T CALL ME DARLING," she screamed. She picked up another item – Russell's fishing rod.

"Oh no you don't!" Russell lunged at her and began prying the rod out of her fingers. "You just get ahold of yourself Edna. You are being ridiculous." She fought him for control of the rod. They continued to wrangle over the rod for a few more moments and Edna finally gave in.

"Fine, take your precious rod," she said in a strange, taunting way. She angrily wiped the tears from her face and plunked down on the back bench seat, staring at Russell, waiting for him to say something. He just looked at her. It was a stand-off. Suddenly she got up, walked right up to Russell and slapped him across the face. "I hate you."

The slap stung. The words didn't. He knew she didn't mean it. He also knew he better get to shore and get her off this boat. He turned from her to start the engine and take the wheel. She flung herself on his back. "Don't you turn away from me!" She was screaming again, pounding her fists on his back. "You stay out here and talk to me."

"Edna, I just think we should head home. Don't you?" Russell was trying so hard to stay calm, but his heart was racing. If she would stop screaming at him, he was sure he would be able to hear it thumping.

"What *I* think… what do you or anyone else care what *I* think?" She began sobbing again and suddenly dropped down to the floor of the craft and began pounding at everything: the floor, the seat cushions, and herself.

Russell started to really panic. He started the engine and raced for shore. Edna still lay on the floor, sobbing, pounding, hitting, and pulling her own hair.

It only took 15 minutes to reach the dock, but it felt like forever. Russell jumped out and ran to the rental office. He threw the keys on the desk and a ten dollar bill. "I have to go. My wife… she's in trouble. I'm sorry." With that he ran back to the boat.

Edna was still on the floor, motionless. He knelt down beside her and pulled the hair back from her face. Her eyes were closed tight, and she was mumbling something, but he couldn't understand it. He listened for a moment, trying to make out what she was saying. It was names: her grandparents, her great-grandparents, and on and on. Almost in a whisper, the names kept coming, one after another.

He gently tried to coax her to get up, but all she did was whimper and continue to mumble more names. Russell crouched down and lifted her up into his arms. Getting out of the boat was no small task. She only weighed all of 125 pounds, even nearly four months pregnant, but he had to step over the side of the boat and out onto the dock. In his desperation, he found the strength to get out of the boat and back to the car, still carrying Edna, who had gone limp.

*   *   *

Ginny heard the car pull into the driveway and shouted, "Mother and Daddy are home!" She ran to greet them at the back porch door. Her mother walked right past her, as if she didn't even see her, and went straight to the bedroom. Her father walked in looking disheveled.

"Daddy, are you alright? What's wrong with Mother?"

Russell slumped the right side of his body against the kitchen door jamb and just looked at Ginny for a moment. "I've been through hell today, Virginia." He staggered into the dining room and sat for a moment at the table, staring at the lace tablecloth.

Before Ginny could think of what to say, she heard the bedroom door open. Edna walked into the room, calmly turned to Ginny and said, "Would you bring me a class of water please, Virginia?" Ginny went to the kitchen to fetch the water while Edna stood still, staring at Russell. She returned and handed Edna the glass. Edna began to slowly raise it to her lips, her eyes still fixed on Russell. Without warning she suddenly threw it. The glass flew across the room right at Russell's head. He quickly ducked to the right and narrowly missed getting hit and the glass shattered against the wall behind him.

As if nothing happened, Edna calmly walked into the living room and sat down on the floor, next to David and Cherie who had been playing with David's blocks, but were now sitting still, unsure of the situation. Suddenly, and for no apparent reason at all, Edna pushed them with great force, knocking them both over, David hitting his head on Cherie's chin. Edna turned to the television, which wasn't turned on, and stared, while David and Cherie both began to cry. Ginny was horrified.

"Mother, what's the matter?" She went to David and scooped him up, hugging him and comforting him.

Edna continued to stare at the blank television screen. Cherie kept crying. David whimpered in Ginny's arms.

Ginny looked at her father, who was still staring at the lace tablecloth. Silently, he got up and went to the corner of the room and picked up the telephone. "Wayne, I need your help. Would you mind coming over immediately?" Pause. "Thank you so much." He made another call and repeated the same thing. Then another and another. He called four friends from church.

It only took about 15 minutes for all four men to arrive. They talked with Russell on the front porch where he had waited for their arrival. Ginny strained to hear what they were saying but could not. The front door opened, they all walked in and stood near Edna, who was still staring at the blank T.V. "Edna," one of them said, "Won't you come for a little ride?" No response. "Edna, we'll go get some See's candy. Now wouldn't that be nice?" No response.

Russell nodded his head at the four of them and they each stepped toward Edna and then Russell took hold of Edna's arm and told her they needed to take her to the sanitarium. Edna yanked her arm away and shrieked at them, "You can't make me go!"

Russell turned to the girls, all becoming distressed about the situation, and told them as calmly as he could to take David and go to their rooms. Deanna and Cherie both began to cry and ran to their rooms. Ginny picked up David from the floor and whispered in his ear that everything was alright while she quietly disappeared down the hall to David's room.

The four men waited until the children were in their rooms and apologetically took Edna by both arms. But Edna flailed about, kicking and screaming and refused to be compliant with their repeated requests for her to simply come with them. All of the men were friends from church and knew the Peak family well yet had never seen Edna behave remotely like this. Concern and anxiety were written all over their faces as they tried, desperately, to convince Edna to calm down. But try as they might, she continued to flail about, screaming at them to leave her alone. They finally had no choice but to also take her legs and hold them tightly; two of the men wrapping their arms around her by the ankles and knees. Russell opened the door for them, ran to the car and opened the door to the back seat. Two of the men sat with Edna and accompanied them to the sanitarium.

Ginny had gone to the window after she heard the front door close and watched as they struggled to get Edna in the car. *What was happening and would her mother be alright?* Ginny's whole body filled with fear and anxiety as she watched the car back out of the driveway and speed off until it was out of sight.

*   *   *

"Someone get him out of here!" the doctor in charge shouted out.

"Mr. Peak, come with us, you'd be better off to wait in the lounge." Two male assistants tried to take his arm and lead him down the hall, but Russell wouldn't go.

"I won't be any trouble, please let me stay with her. She needs to know I'm here," Russell pleaded.

"She's not even fully aware of what's happening to her Mr. Peak, and you wouldn't want to see the treatments she has to get. The doctor is going to do it immediately," one of the assistants responded.

Russell had rushed up to the emergency entrance of Rock Haven Sanitarium only moments ago. At first Edna seemed unconscious, slumped over in the back seat. But as they tried to coax her to wake up and step out of the car, she began to act wildly again, screaming, mumbling, crying, and thrashing at anyone who tried to pull her from the car.

They had quickly given Edna a sedative to calm her and she was finally still as they wheeled her to a treatment room, mumbling incoherently but not thrashing about any longer.

Russell once again pleaded with the two assistants to let him be in the treatment room with Edna. Reluctantly agreeing, they walked down a long hallway to treatment room 110 and once inside Russell quietly stood in the corner, going unnoticed by the doctor who was already busy attaching pads to Edna's temples and what looked like a large clamp contraption to her forehead. A nurse stuffed a white cloth into Edna's mouth and held her chin closed while another nurse held Edna's forehead down. The doctor turned to a machine next to her bed and turned a dial that made a clicking noise, then he flipped a switch. Edna threw her head back and the nurse struggled to keep it held down to the bed, then the rest of her body began to convulse. Edna let out a loud moan and her limbs began to shake. They all calmly watched and waited for the fit to ebb.

Russell was horrified. "Oh please, dear God help her," he cried out and began to sob. He knew of the treatments but had never seen one. It was more than he could bear.

The assistant closest to him gently said once again, "Mr. Peak, why don't you wait in the lounge. I'll come and get you when it's all over." He put a hand on Russell's shoulder and led him out of the room.

*   *   *

Russell nervously walked into Edna's room after about an hour. She was lying on her back, sleeping. He walked up to her and gazed down at her face. She looked pale and there were two faint burn marks on each side of her forehead where the pads had been attached. He picked up one of her hands in his and whispered, "I love you." It was emotionally painful to see her lying there, so frail and helpless. Russell pulled his handkerchief from his pocket and dabbed at his eyes.

Edna stirred and slowly opened her eyes. She stared for a moment at Russell and finally said in a frightened tone, "Who are you? Why are you here? Where am I?" Her eyes were wide as she looked around the room at her strange surroundings. She jerked her hand out of his.

"Edna darling, you're at Rock Haven Sanitarium. You've been here before. Can't you remember it?" Russell paused, "And I'm

Russell," he looked at her with pleading eyes, "Your husband." She just stared at him with a look of utter disbelief and unrecognition.

"I don't know you and I would feel better if you left. Please." She looked at him and waited.

There was nothing he could do but leave, so he sorrowfully turned and walked out of her room. He found the doctor in the hall with a nurse who had assisted him with Edna's treatment. "May I have a word with you, privately?" Russell asked him.

"Certainly, Mr. Peak. Why don't you come to my office where we can talk?" Russell nodded in agreement and followed the doctor to a simple, yet comfortable office. The doctor took a seat behind his desk and motioned for Russell to sit down opposite him. "I know this is very difficult for you Mr. Peak. You understand that don't you?"

"Yes."

"Then what can I help you with?"

"I understand that memory loss is usually a side effect of electric shock treatment. If they forget something, can they, or, well, *will* they ever remember it again? Or is the memory gone for good?" Russell's eyes glazed over with fear, emotion, and sadness.

"That depends. Sometimes they forget things permanently. We've found it to be a benefit at times though; when a patient is able to forget a traumatic experience. For example, most of the time, luckily, they have very little memory of the shock treatment procedure.

"What about people?"

"People?"

"Yes. Can they permanently forget a person?" Russell tried to maintain his composure, but it was difficult. His entire future depended on the doctor's answer.

"Are you referring to yourself, Mr. Peak?" the doctor asked with sincere compassion.

Russell looked down at his hands in his lap and replied quietly, "Yes. She doesn't remember me."

The doctor looked at Russell for a moment before choosing his words carefully. "Mr. Peak, the chances are very slim that she has permanently forgotten who you are. It would be highly unusual for a patient to forget their spouse." He paused for a moment, then asked, "How long have you been married?"

"Seventeen years. To the day."

14

April 21, 1952

THERE WAS A stack of untouched books next to Edna's bed. She looked over at them and saw a note perched on top and knew immediately they were from Russell, but she simply looked away.

Russell had brought them early that morning. He walked quietly into her room and when he looked at Edna, she only stared at the wall, not making any indication she even noticed him entering the room. He had no idea where her mind was, or if she even remembered who he was yet, so he thought it best to simply leave the books with his note sitting on top.

She still hadn't read the note.

Edna closed her eyes. She could see her mother's coffin. It was there, at the funeral parlor. There was a plant... a fern... sitting next to it on a stand. She was walking towards it, with her father and two brothers, hating the fact that it was her dear mother lying there – dead. Edna had just turned 18 and had been planning on going to college but her mother suddenly fell ill and two weeks later she had died. Her mother looked beautiful in a green dress that ————————

she had made for herself just the year before. She had made Dale, Edna's youngest brother, a vest out of the remaining fabric. Paul, who was turning 16 in two weeks, walked in with his arm around Edna, trying to comfort her; and himself. Edna was holding Dale's hand when he suddenly let go and ran up to the casket, crying out pitifully, "Mother!" Edna began to sob. Her father sobbed. Paul squeezed her shoulder tighter and whispered in her ear something... she couldn't make it out. The crying was too loud. It was getting louder, and louder...

Edna opened her eyes with a start. A nurse suddenly appeared in the room.

"Mrs. Peak, what's wrong?"

Edna stared at her, confused.

"You were crying. Are you alright? Would you like me to get the doctor?"

Edna still lay there, staring at the nurse. She didn't know this woman, or where she was, exactly. She looked around, scanning the walls and the room. It all seemed familiar, but...

"Can I get you something to eat? You haven't eaten anything since you've been here. You must be hungry Mrs. Peak." The nurse came to her bedside and waited for Edna to reply.

Edna remained silent, looking at her. The nurse waited a few moments, patted her hand and finally left the room. E dna could hear talking out in the hall. She knew the nurse was talking about her.

People always talked about her. Just after mother died... the church they went to... in the chapel, all the wooden pews filled with people, whispering as she and her father and brothers walked in. A rather plump woman with a silly little pink hat came up to Edna and said in a high, shrill voice how sorry she was about her mother and that she would come help Edna with the house and cooking. Her breath was awful. Edna hated her. She had seen this very woman, just a few moments ago, talking about her. She was probably telling everyone that Edna couldn't possibly take care of the household. She could still hear whispering. The preacher began to speak, but she couldn't hear him over all the whispering... about HER.

Edna's mind was suddenly back in her room at Rock Haven Sanitarium. A doctor and two nurses were whispering something to each other when they noticed Edna staring at them. "Mrs. Peak, we're going to take you into the treatment room now."

Edna looked over in the corner of the room. She saw someone standing there. It was the little fat woman from church in her pink hat. Edna shouted "Leave! Get out. I don't want you in here. I can keep the house by myself, we don't need you."

The doctor looked in the corner where Edna was directing her shouting. "Mrs. Peak, there's no one there." He nodded at the nurses who took hold of Edna's bed and began rolling her out of the room.

Edna kept her eyes fixed on the woman in the pink hat who was smiling a sly and wicked smile at her. Edna sneered back at her and again said, "Leave me alone!"

Once in the treatment room, Edna lay still while they attached the pads, the clamp, and put the rag into her mouth. She felt nurses hold her chin and her forehead and heard the clicking noise from the machine next to her bed.

*   *   *

Russell visited again that evening after he left the store. He walked into Edna's room and looked down at her while she slept. Even in the dim light he could see fresh burn marks on her temples. The nurse at the front desk had told Russell that she would most likely be asleep and wouldn't wake up until the next morning. Fine. He just wanted to see her.

15

May 6, 1952

WE JUST DON'T feel we can do anything more for her Mr. Peak. She's been here for more than two weeks and we thought she was making some progress until a few days ago when she became depressed, angry, paranoid, despondent, violent – "

"I understand," Russell interrupted him. He really couldn't stand to hear the list. "What am I to do? I can't take her home; at least not yet." Russell rubbed his chin with his hands as he thought about the prospect of Edna returning home in her condition. "She could hurt one of the children."

"Mr. Peak, might I suggest that she be transferred to Braeburn Sanitarium. They have slightly more sophisticated machines and their doctors are very well educated and have more experience with the degree of illness that your wife has. They will be able to give her more shock treatments with better results, I think." After an uncomfortable pause he continued, "They are also much closer to the hospital where..." The doctor shifted in his chair, "She may need medical attention for the loss of the pregnancy. You understand that, don't you Mr. Peak?"

Russell barely managed to nod his head. It broke him up when they told him Edna had lost the baby. He was devastated when they told him that it had been a boy. The evening he had received the news, he had to pull over on the way home from his shop to weep.

Continuing, the doctor said, "I'm very sorry. I know this has contributed to your wife's difficulty in making her recovery. The pregnancy itself may have contributed to her initial breakdown as well." Sitting forward in his chair, he looked at Russell who was just staring back at him, blankly, in a daze. "I really think if Edna...*when* Edna recovers, it would be a very good idea for you to try and spend a little more time with her. Maybe take her someplace special every Friday night, just the two of you. It would be something she could count on and look forward to." The doctor paused and waited for Russell to respond. Russell only faintly nodded. "I'm not suggesting it would keep her from ever becoming ill again, I just think it would help."

Nodding his head more firmly Russell said, "I'll do anything to help my wife."

"I know you would, Mr. Peak. I know you would. Please don't think that her condition is your fault. This sort of thing usually runs in families. I understand she has a brother who suffers from depression, is that right?"

"Yes, her brother Paul."

"Well, she is fortunate to have such long periods of time that she feels reasonably well." Taking out a file from his desk drawer he continued, "Now, about the transfer to Braeburn - I will need you to fill out some papers and our facility will make the necessary arrangements to transport her there, if it is agreeable to you, Mr. Peak?"

Feeling numb, Russell agreed to the transfer and mechanically began to fill out the paperwork. After a few moments he asked, "Is Braeburn going to be more expensive?"

"Their daily fees are only a little higher than here. I'm not sure how the doctors' fees compare." Looking thoughtfully at Russell he added, "I think they will work with you on payments, Mr. Peak."

"Oh… well… I have savings. I just wondered how the cost was going to compare, that's all," Russell turned his attention back to the clipboard with the papers he was filling out. He did have savings. This was probably going to wipe it out. He would just have to save again. He would do anything to help Edna.

16

July – February 1953

E DNA WAS IN Rock Haven and Braeburn Sanitariums for two
months. It had been very difficult on the family, but they
had friends, neighbors, and especially family who had shown
them so much kindness. They had brought them meals, watched
David, helped the girls with schoolwork, taken them to lessons and
even done laundry, dishes, dusting, vacuuming, and polishing. The
three girls had managed to maintain their good grades in school
despite the worries over their mother and the extra chores.

David, on the other hand, had had a very hard time of it all. He
was just a little three-year old when it happened. His whole world
depended on routine. He didn't even like it if a piece of furniture got
moved from its usual place. He would walk around it and around it,
mumbling and running his fingers through his hair until someone
finally moved it back to its original spot.

Every day he would say with pleading, questioning eyes,
"Muthuh?" And every day, whoever was watching him would try
to explain to him in a way they only hoped he could understand,

"Your mother is sick, David. She'll be alright and home in no time, I'm sure." He would just stare at whoever and say again, "Muthuh?" Sometimes he would cry and rock himself back and forth. He even began a peculiar habit of clacking his teeth. Russell became worried over the terrible habit and took him to the dentist who said that he would most likely quit when his mother returned home, and life was once again back to normal. Not to worry.

Bedtime was especially trying. Whoever had been there helping and watching David during the day would return to their own home shortly after the girls came home from school. Ginny would usually get dinner out for everyone and Deanna and Cherie would clean the kitchen. Russell tried very hard to come home before they were all in bed to give them kisses and hugs and to try and help with David, who would usually begin throwing a fit as soon as someone said, "It's bedtime Davie." He would scream, "Muthuh! Muthuh!" Edna had always given him a nice warm bath every night, so Ginny would try to get him to take a bath. Sometimes it worked, other times it didn't. The one thing he seemed to like that would actually soothe him was if Ginny would take out her violin and play for him. He would suddenly stop screaming and would just sit and rock and clack his teeth. Then he would get drowsy and Deanna or Cherie would come along and hold him and finally carry him into their parents' room and put him in his crib. This was tiresome for the girls every night after their own usual activities of school and homework. But they managed. Russell managed. Even poor little Davie managed.

*　　*　　*

For the whole summer after Edna came home, she was still sad every day and battled feeling depressed. She didn't even enjoy the family vacation to Yellowstone that year. But in the fall, when the routine of the school year started, she began to perk up a bit, and then Christmas really did the trick. Edna was back! And she seemed better than ever. She was noticeably more patient and tolerant. One day David had broken a vase that she particularly cared for and she hardly even seemed to notice, let-alone get upset over it. She simply swept up the pieces and threw them in the trash. Nothing seemed to bother her.

Russell was as calm and patient as he had ever been. Only once during the whole ordeal did he lose his temper. And it was over a couple of silly roosters. He had bought two bantam roosters for their feathers, to make flies out of them for the store. The two roosters hated each other and were continually fighting – and ruining their feathers in the process. One day, Russell had had it! So, he took a gunny sack from the cellar, marched outside, his face red with anger, grabbed one of the roosters and stuffed it into the bag. Russell chased down the other rooster and managed to get a hold of it, all the while clinging to the sack with the squawking rooster inside. After a terrible struggle to stuff it into the sack, Russell clenched the bag shut with both hands and SHOOK it! He shook it as hard and furiously as he could, yelling, and calling them names as he shook.

When he finally stopped, he was out of breath. He sat down in a chair and let the bag fall to the ground. The bag lay still for quite some time while Russell sat, arms dangling at the sides of the chair and his head flopped over against his chest, exhausted. Then the bag moved and the roosters slowly immerged, staggering around the yard like a couple of drunks.

But they never fought again.

*   *   *

Almost a whole year had passed by, and life seemed wonderful again. The family never talked about the two awful months anymore. They hardly ever even thought about it. They had not only survived the difficulties but had grown closer as a result of their hardship.

One day Edna was driving the four children to the park and Virginia was sitting in the front seat with David standing on the seat between her and Edna – his usual spot.

Virginia looked at his hand dangling at his side, and picking it up in hers asked, "Mother, why is Davie's little finger bent like that?"

Edna was taken a little off her guard by the question. She and Russell had never discussed anything about Davie's condition with the girls. "Because he was born a mongoloid baby," she said matter-of-factly.

"What does that mean? A 'mongoloid'?" Virginia asked.

"Well, it means that he has some unusual characteristics."

"Like what?"

Edna wondered for a moment how Ginny would feel about her brother if she knew he wasn't normal. "Well, for instance how his eyes look. And how short his fingers are. And… how he learns a little slower than most children. Things like that."

Edna was actually surprised at herself. David was now 4 years old and for the last 4 years whenever she discussed his condition, she had to fight crying about it. But not this time. She didn't even feel like crying. Ginny didn't seem to be concerned either. She just said, "Oh," and that was that. The other two girls were busy giggling and talking in the back seat and didn't seem to hear any of the conversation. Edna wondered if they would ever notice how their brother was different and also ask about it. *Everything will be just fine if they do*, thought Edna.

17

November 16, 1953

ODAY WAS A big day. David was starting school! Russell and Edna had discussed schooling for David shortly before Edna's breakdown, but neither one of them had had any idea what they were going to do about it. Public schools did not accept children with conditions like David's and they didn't know of any other schools he could attend.

Then a miracle happened. A woman Edna met one day while at the bookstore was very interested in David and asked about him. She said that she had a son whom she had also been told had mongolism. He was just one year older than David and she said she was thinking about teaching three other mongoloid children she knew of out of her home. She wanted to know if Edna and Russell would be interested in having David come to her little home school. They had exchanged phone numbers and a few days later Edna had called her.

And now here they were. Edna felt a little nervous, but Russell had reminded her just that morning before heading off to his shop that this was a very good opportunity for David. She knew that, but it was hard to imagine leaving David somewhere she was so unfamiliar with. She had never left him at anyone's home before.

Edna held David's hand as she knocked on the door. They were greeted warmly by Mrs. Keith, "Good morning Edna, I'm so happy to have you and David here. Won't you please come in." Edna followed her into the living room with David clinging to her hand. Mrs. Keith squat down in front of David and took his other hand in hers as she said, "David, we have some really fun and special things planned for today! Right now, you can do whatever you want: you can play with toys or watch TV or eat a snack." She stood up and continued, "Your mother will stay right here until you feel ready."

Edna looked around the room, noticing first how Mrs. Keith had rearranged her furniture to accommodate the needs of the children and to create a learning atmosphere. There was a chalk-board on an easel in front of the fireplace and five desk and chair sets set up facing it. Games and toys were organized in a set of shelves separating the living room and dining room and the dining room table had several stacks of books in the center.

Edna looked around at the four children, two boys and two girls, who were all busily doing different things to occupy themselves. It was so odd – to see children who looked like David. They all had the same eyes and round faces and their tongues protruded from their mouths just like David's always did. One of the girls was a little pudgy thing and was sitting on the floor trying to put a puzzle together. She had kept trying piece after piece until she found one that fit. She appeared to Edna to be around 9 or 10 years old. The other girl looked a year or two younger and was sitting on the couch reading a book. Edna chuckled to herself as she noticed that the book was upside down. The two boys were at the table coloring, one of them was Mrs. Keith's son who was the oldest child in the group and the other looked about David's age. They were both bent down with their faces so close to the paper that their noses almost touched it. The younger little boy kept glancing over at Mrs. Keith's son, making sure to imitate everything he did.

David let go of Edna's hand and walked up to the two boys. He stood at the table, staring at their papers and the bright colored crayons. The older boy looked startled to see David as if he had magically appeared before him, but his mouth became a broad smile and he loudly said, "Hi! I'm Danny!" He stuck out his hand to shake David's, but David had never shook anyone's hand before so he just stared at it. Danny kept smiling at David and reached down, took David's hand into his, shook it up and down about 20 times and loudly said, "There, like that." He finally let go and pulled out the chair next to him and said, "Sit." David immediately sat in the chair and the boy put a piece of paper and a handful of crayons in front of him and commanded in the same loud voice, "Color."

Edna watched David from where she still stood near the door, amazed. Maybe this was going to work out just fine. David seemed to be perfectly content and comfortable. Mrs. Keith apologetically explained, "Danny is hard-of-hearing, so he is rather loud. His doctor said it's quite common in mongoloid children." She and Edna watched David for a moment then Mrs. Keith continued, "Your son and Bobby Durfee are close to the same age. Bobby's 5, almost 6, and David is almost 5, is that correct Mrs. Peak?"

Edna nodded her head and said, "Yes, that's right, in January he'll be 5."

"You are welcome to stay today for a while if you would like, but David seems to be getting along just fine, doesn't he?"

"I'm quite surprised," Edna replied happily, "I thought he would have a rather difficult time of it. This is such a new experience for him." They watched David and Bobby and Danny color, all three hunched over their papers, making random streaks of color and switching crayons every few seconds. Edna continued, "If David becomes troublesome, please phone me and I'll come as quickly as I can."

Mrs. Keith looked at Edna compassionately and said reassuringly, "Oh, I'm sure he'll be just fine. Gracie, Arlene, and Bobby are the most delightful children. They will play nicely together. I'm certain." Mrs. Keith gestured toward her son and added, "Danny is always trying to take care of everyone; he's my only child so school is his big opportunity to feel like he has brothers and sisters."

Edna sat down on the couch and Mrs. Keith moved around amongst the children, commenting to Arlene that she was doing an excellent job with her puzzle, taking the book gently from Gracie's hands and flipping it right-side-up, then visiting with the three boys at the table and asking them questions about their drawings. Edna's heart wanted to thump out of her chest she was so pleased with everything about David's new "school." *What an incredible blessing and opportunity that has nearly fallen right into our laps!* Edna thought as she watched the scene before her.

After about 20 minutes Edna finally decided she could leave without worrying. Calling David to come to her she said, "Give mother a kiss Davie Dear." Bending down to receive it, she tried to put her arms around him for a hug as well but he wiggled free and ran back to Danny and Bobby. "Well! I guess he doesn't need *me* anymore!" Edna laughed to Mrs. Keith and then said goodbye and left.

*　　*　　*

Edna picked up David later that afternoon. He ran to her shouting, "Muthuh! Muthuh!" and proudly held up a stick with a paper bird attached to it by a long string. "Burdth!" he proudly exclaimed.

"That's right, Davie! It's a beautiful bird! Did you make it here at school today?"

"Burdth," he repeated and ran around the room with the stick held above his head, the bird fluttering as if it were flying.

"Wonderful Davie! I see why you love it so much." Edna watched as David continued to run around with the stick over his head. "Daddy will be so pleased to see it when he gets home tonight. Come along now, say goodbye to your new friends and your teacher."

"Bah-bay," he said to the room in general and he took Edna's hand to go.

Once at home Edna turned on the television to entertain David while she prepared dinner. The girls came home from school and she could hear them enthusiastically complimenting David's new bird. They were always so very sweet to their baby brother. She could hear the television's program – the New York Symphony, and thought David might get bored of it quickly so she went to the living room to change the channel. David was sitting on the floor, a foot away from the TV, looking mesmerized. So she decided to leave well-enough alone and went back to the kitchen. The girls came in and began to tell Edna about their school activities of the day and asked her for help with homework. She cooked, listened, and helped. Suddenly David jumped up from his spot in front of the television, ran into the kitchen and opened the oven door. *What in heaven's name is he doing?* Edna wondered. She and the girls had all stopped what they were doing to watch David. He gripped the baking rack with both hands, yanked it out of the oven, and ran back to his spot on the living room floor. He held up the rack with his left hand and then began strumming it with his right hand.

"Well, I'll-be-darned," Edna said out loud, "It's a harp!" She and the girls stood and watched David strum his harp as the symphony on the television played. David was a harpist in a symphony.

That night, lying in bed, Edna thought about how well David was doing and how curious he was. He was learning so much; his vocabulary was growing, and he could say nearly 30 or so words now. They had successfully toilet-trained him that summer and it was wonderful not to have all those diapers to wash and hang on the line anymore. And how smart he must be, to be so fascinated by a *symphony,* she thought. And then to have such imagination to use the oven rack as a harp! She felt so happy, so proud of him, so hopeful. Edna lay in the dark, excited for morning when she could tell Russell all about it. He still wasn't home from the shop and she was too tired to wait up for him any longer. *School is going to be such a wonderful thing for Davie,* she thought as she drifted off to sleep.

18

July 11, 1954

THE SUMMER'S FAMILY vacation to Montana promised to be everything the family was hoping for. Edna's breakdown was so far behind them now that time had done a nice job of healing their wounds.

David especially had been enjoying the long two-day drive. He had been learning his colors in school that year and had entertained himself the entire drive by calling out every color he saw. "Green! Blue! Green! Green! White! White!" The family got tired of every green tree and every white cloud and tried to get him to notice more obscure things with different colors such as road signs, passing cars, and buildings. David continued to call out every green tree, every white cloud, and the blue sky.

Halfway through the second day, Russell drove through the gate of a sprawling horse ranch. The day was perfect for a horseback ride and the family was excited to go. While Russell made arrangements with one of the ranch hands, Edna and the girls prepared sandwiches for a picnic lunch. They were just south of Yellowstone National Park where they would camp later that night.

"Where do you suggest we go?" Russell asked the fellow helping him. "Is there a trail we should follow?"

The ranch hand, wearing a plaid shirt, cowboy hat, cowboy boots, jeans and a belt with a large silver buckle, pointed to the south side of the ranch and said, "I'd take the trail that starts just at the end of that corral over there and follow it as far as the clearing on the other side of that hill. You can ride them horses all day long and they'll do whatever you want them to." He put his thumbs in his jeans' pockets and continued, "Just be careful coming back, they get a bit excited and want to run home."

"Will do. How much do we owe you?"

"We can settle that up when you get back – it'll depend on how long you're gone for," the ranch hand said, then looked at David who was standing a few yards away from them, looking at the horses in a fenced-in grassy area. "You better make sure that boy of yours don't go near them horses over there. They ain't broke yet and they don't care for people much, let-alone a boy like yours." He paused as he stared at David, then added, "If he got in there bothering them, one kick could kill him."

Russell felt angry at his inference about David, but decided to simply say, "Okay." Walking over to David, he took his hand and led him back over to the car where a picnic lunch was ready. "Should be a grand ride on these trails. That fellow said that just this morning they had a rider spot a black bear over there, just past that group of hills!" Russell pointed out the area he was talking about and excitedly asked, "Wouldn't that be fun to see a bear?" He got mixed opinions from the four womenfolk about seeing a bear, nevertheless, they were all excited about the horseback ride.

Under the shade of a large oak tree, a blessing on the food was offered, and the family chattered as they dove into their lunch, satisfying their hunger. A very gentle breeze kept them perfectly comfortable in the shade and the scenery was breathtaking. In the distance were rolling hills, and behind them were pine trees with patches of birch and aspens mixed amongst them. The ranch looked like something from a Roy Rogers movie. "Oh girls, look over there, near that big red barn," Edna exclaimed, and everyone looked in the direction she was pointing.

"Oh mother, how cute!" Deanna said, "It's a mamma horse and her baby!"

As they continued eating their sandwiches, pickles, and chips, they all watched the baby nuzzle its mother's belly searching for milk as the mother stood still and patient. It was a beautiful and perfect scene that captured their attention until Ginny asked, "Can animals be mongoloids, Mother?"

Edna's eyes shot up at Deanna and Cherie. They still had not asked anything about David's unusual characteristics, so Edna had never said anything to them about it. At the moment, she was regretting that decision.

Ginny, Deanna, and Cherie looked back at Edna, waiting for her answer.

"Well dear, what an interesting question." Edna shifted her weight and put down her sandwich. "I have never thought about it. But..." Edna gave the question some quick, impromptu thought, then replied, "I really wouldn't imagine so. I think it must be one of those things that only humans have." Edna looked at Deanna and Cherie again. They simply looked over at the tiny dark brown foal and its mother and kept eating their sandwiches. "Girls, I explained to Ginny one day that David is a mongoloid and –"

"We know, Mother," Cherie cut her off, "Ginny told us all about it! She said that's why David's tongue sticks out and why his little finger is bent, and she said that's why he's so cute."

The innocence and love of children is a beautiful thing, Edna thought, as her heart was touched by her daughter's words. She felt comforted knowing that the girls loved their little brother just as he was.

Edna's happy thoughts were interrupted by Russell who suddenly put his sandwich down and asked, "Where is David?" Distracted by the mother and foal and Ginny's question, they hadn't noticed David wander off.

"He must be right around here somewhere, Darling. He was just here a moment ago." Edna set her sandwich down and began scanning their surroundings.

Russell hardly even heard what Edna said. He looked over at the fenced-in corral to the west. He couldn't see David but felt nervous. He jumped up and began to run toward the fence. As he got closer, he saw David's red jacket flicker in between the horses. He watched in horror as David squat down and worked his way *under* one of the horse's belly. Then David weaved in and out of them, brushing his hands along their hindquarters and running his hands through their tail hair. Russell was horrified and froze in his tracks for a moment, his heart beating against his chest and his stomach feeling almost sick. Then he ran as fast as he could to the fence. "David, you absolutely must leave those horses alone and come out of there. Now!" He tried to sound calm, but he didn't feel calm at all. Should he jump in and grab him? What if that set the horses off? They didn't actually seem to be bothered by David in the least.

David looked up at Russell, his hand still stroking one of the horses. He leaned over and kissed the animal and then walked toward Russell. "I coming Fathuh," he said, and then he took the most direct route back to Russell which was back *under* two horses' bellies. Russell thought he was going to have a heart attack. He prayed in his heart, "Dear God, keep those horses calm. Just keep them calm."

David had a big smile on his face as he reached the fence. "Hortheth!" he exclaimed happily, "brown." Russell hugged him tight and kissed his cheeks. "I like hortheth Fathuh!"

*   *   *

Russell stood knee-deep in the cool, clear, rushing water. The family had made it to their campsite the evening before and he and Edna had come to the river early to fish while the sun made its way up. There was an orange and pink glow emanating from the east, peeking through the snow-capped Rocky Mountain range in the distance. The river flowed over rocks, creating a very gentle rushing sound, and the brush along the banks was perfectly still, as if they hadn't woken up yet. Birds were cheerfully calling to one another, providing a soft noise that announced the new day. Casting his rod back and forth, he took a long, deep breath of fresh air.

Edna was also knee-deep just a few yards away. They loved to fish together. They could spend hours in silence, just casting away, not feeling the need to say anything. Nature is perfect in the silence. Sometimes he and Edna talked plenty, usually about the children, church, the latest book Edna was reading, or the goings-on at the store. Today was the perfect day for just thinking.

After the scare the day before with the horse episode, Russell was feeling especially thoughtful. How badly he could be feeling if just one of those horses had decided not to be patient with his little son; Russell didn't even want to think about it. *David must have guardian angels all around him,* Russell thought. *It is a full-time job for them to keep him out of trouble and safe.* Russell chuckled to himself at the thought of tiny David escorted everywhere he went by a flock of angels with their arms outstretched around him, desperately trying to keep him from going where he shouldn't go in the first place, then finally raising their angel arms in despair as he climbed through the fence anyway. Then he pictured them, all in white, stroking the horses over and over and whispering in their ears, "Stay still, you mustn't move. Stay still," while David weaved his way under their bellies and through their legs. Russell breathed in another deep breath, glanced over at Edna, and smiled at the thought that angels had saved David. Again.

19

January 30, 1955

DAVID HAD LIVED to see another birthday, despite his obstacle course through a heard of wild horses, and today was his 6th. Edna had decided it was time to throw him a real birthday party since he had been in school for over a year now and had made several good friends. She had invited them all to come: Arlene, Danny, Gracie, and Bobby, who had become David's close buddy, and two new students: Owen and… Oh, why couldn't she remember her name? Such a darling little girl, the youngest of the bunch. None of them were shy and they all had infectious smiles and loved to hug. They hugged each other every day as they arrived at Mrs. Keith's home for school. She had asked Mrs. Keith a couple weeks ago about another student, whom David continually talked about, named Sally, wanting to be sure and invite her to David's party. But Mrs. Keith insisted that she didn't have a student named Sally.

Just that Morning Edna had overheard David talking in his room. When she came closer to try and make out what he was saying she heard David say, "Sally, my buthday! Sally, cake! My buthday!" She carefully peeked around the door jamb, hoping he wouldn't catch her spying on him. He was standing in the middle of his room, facing the wall where his dresser stood, and he was rocking back and forth just a little. Then he reached up, put his hand in the air directly in front of himself and made stroking motions, as if he were touching someone's face. Edna realized that "Sally" was an imaginary friend.

Edna and the girls had decorated the back yard with colorful balloons and paper chains that Deanna and Cherie had made for the occasion. The kumquat tree was still full of the glossy, bright orange fruit and looked quite festive. Edna and the girls had baked a large cake and decorated it with bright colored frosting, and it sat in the center of the picnic table with gifts the other children had brought. As the children arrived, they each found toys to play with and balls to bounce on the patio cement. There was chatter and laughter as Ginny, Deanna, Cherie, and all the children played. All except David, who stood at the picnic table, staring at the cake.

"Davie Darling, please go play with your friends, they are all here to be with you."

David looked up at Edna thoughtfully, then simply said, "Cake."

Edna looked at the cake in the center of the table and realized that all David wanted to do was eat cake. Nothing else was enticing and she doubted he could be talked in to any other activity until he was able to eat cake. "Children," she hollered, "Children come to the table. We are going to eat the cake." She looked back down at David and smiled. David smiled a huge grin at her and eagerly sat down on the bench, putting his little hands on the spot next to him that he was saving for Sally. He kept saying, "Sally here," and patted the spot on the bench with his hand. Looking at the picnic table full of children she felt so pleased that they had met Mrs. Keith and that he had all these *real* friends to enjoy his birthday with, even despite insisting that no one sit right next to him.

After cake, David began opening his presents, holding each new treasure up over his head for all to see and then getting up and hugging the gift-giver. Edna and Russell waited until the last gift was opened to present him with their special gift. David ripped open the paper and looked at a rather large box. He was thrilled! He jumped up and ran to his mother and father to thank them. They laughed and hugged him and then Russell said, "David, the present isn't the box, the present is *in* the box!"

David stared at him for a moment, as if he didn't understand, then said, "*In* the bockth."

"Yes David, *In* the box."

David ran back to the picnic table and carefully opened the box and stared inside for a moment, then his face was overtaken again by his smile. He clapped his hands and raised them in the air with joy and ran over to his mother and father once again and threw his arms around their necks.

It was a violin. He loved the violin. Ginny used to play but had decided she actually hated it. So, she quit, and they had sold her violin. David had missed it tremendously and wearied them with his constant mutterings, "Ginny, vialin. Ginny, vialin! I wahn Ginny, vialin." So, Russell had bought an old one he ran across at a yard sale, took it to his shop and meticulously refinished its old, worn wood, polished the fingerboard, and re-strung it. He had even carved David's name in tiny letters on the back. It looked wonderful.

For days after the party David spent every moment "playing" his new instrument. He would play and play. He sounded awful. Edna and Russell sometimes had to go outside so they couldn't hear it. It squeaked and squealed out the most wretched sounds. But David loved it.

Ginny, Deanna, and Cherie hated it too. They asked their parents if they could get rid of it as soon as he lost interest in it. Sometimes when he started up again the girls would all start playing the piano together. Battle of the musical instruments. David would play louder. The girls played louder. Edna and Russell would go for a walk.

"Russell darling, do you think he will ever actually learn how to play that thing properly?"

"I think *he* thinks he already does!" Russell replied with a laugh.

"Did I tell you that the other day he was playing for Sally?" Edna asked as she took Russell's hand. "He kept saying 'Sally, listen to this!' It was so comical. I had to duck away so I could laugh without him hearing me." As they walked down the sidewalk, the evening sky was beginning to glow as the sun set lower. They strolled down to Colorado Boulevard, then turned back toward home.

David continued for years to "play" his violin. Not one note ever sounded good. He even began singing along with his playing. Eventually the family became accustomed to hearing it. Occasionally Ginny would try to teach him how to place his hands, how to move the bow properly, and even where a few notes were. She finally thought that if she could just get him to play the A string and the E string without putting his fingers on the fingerboard at all, it would sound alright. But he wouldn't do it. He simply had to pretend that he could play like a virtuoso.

*   *   *

A few days after the birthday party the whole family was treated to a private tour of the amazing new amusement park called "Disney Land." Russell's friend, Ken Anderson, had met them at the entrance and showed them around. It was fascinating. They were all so impressed by the attention to every tiny detail that had been put into everything from the store fronts on Main Street to the signs on the bathroom doors. The park was scheduled to open to the public sometime that summer.

A few of the rides were being tested, so Ken took them on the one he said was going to be the most popular. It was a ride called, "It's a Small World." The family loved it. David adored it. He had a little fit after they emerged back into the sunlight at the end of the ride and so Ken told them they could just stay in the boat and go on it as many times as they liked. They went 17 times. The girls began to moan after about the ninth time and finally Edna and Russell permitted them to get off and look around by themselves with the agreement to meet them back on Main Street in one hour. David began to squeal, "Again, again," as soon as the girls ran off.

By the end of the day, the entire family, David included, sang, "It's a world of laughter, a world of tears, it's a world of hopes and a world of fears. There's so much that we share, that it's time we're aware, it's a small world after all." Then they joined in loudly together, "IT'S A SMALL WORLD AFTER ALL.." over and over they sang as they skipped through the park. It was funny until hours later when they were driving home, and they all had the song stuck in their heads. They blamed David, who slept peacefully the entire way home, stretched out in his usual spot, with his head on Russell's lap and his feet on Edna's.

20

February 1958

THE FRONT DOOR of Russell's store opened causing the bell to tinkle its sound in the air as Russell worked at the counter tying a fly. He looked up to greet the man who was there by appointment. Russell saw customers by appointment only during the week, the store being open to the general public only on Saturdays. The man walked in confidently, extended his hand and introduced himself as John Townsend. Russell introduced himself and asked if he would look around for a moment while he finished the fly in his hand. Mr. Townsend walked over to the wall of custom rods and lightly ran his hands down a few of them. Russell could hear a whispered, "wow."

Russell finished the fly and joined Mr. Townsend at the rods. "Those are a small sampling of what I do, but I assure you I can make anything your client wishes me to," Russell said. "Where does your client like to fish?"

"When he can get away, he usually fishes at Cunningham Falls State Park, mostly because it's closer to his office than other places."

"Oh, I see. Where does he work?"

"The White House."

Russell looked at Mr. Townsend. He thought he must be joking and let out a small chuckle.

Mr. Townsend looked straight at Russell and let him squirm for a moment and then said, "President Eisenhower has heard of your quality craftsmanship. He was told there is none finer and therefore he insisted that I come and discuss his desires to have you make a rod for him."

"My goodness," Russell replied and looked down at his shoes for a moment. Such old, worn shoes. Why hadn't he worn his nicer shoes today? If he had only known he would be taking an order for the President of the United States, he would have come looking more... more professional... or something. "Does he know exactly what he wants?" It was the first question he asked everyone. It felt so unusual to ask a question about the President as if he were a common customer.

"He said he trusts you."

Russell laughed nervously. He couldn't help himself. Dwight D. Eisenhower trusted *him*, Russ Peak!

*   *   *

Russell was too excited to stay late at the store that evening, so he was home in time for dinner, anxious to tell Edna and the girls about his next custom rod and who it was for.

"Goodness gracious Darling, that's wonderful!" exclaimed Edna.

"How exciting Daddy! Do you think we'll meet the president?" asked Cherie.

"No dear. It's an honor to make him a rod though. Maybe when I send it to him you girls can each enclose a nice letter with it. How would that be?"

"Dear, what kind of special things are you going to do to the president's fishing rod? Have you thought about it?" Edna asked.

"I haven't been able to think about anything else all day!" Russell said as he helped himself to a rather large portion of mashed potatoes. "I think I've decided on 5 gold stars inlaid into the rod, and a gold band on the grip."

"How lovely! I'm certain the president will be very pleased indeed."

Cherie asked, "What are the 5 gold stars for Daddy?"

"Because President Eisenhower is a 5-star general!"

The family was so light-hearted during dinner they almost forgot to turn on the television for their favorite program *The Red Skelton Show.* When they left the dinner table for the living room and turned on the TV, David was already plunked down on the floor in front of it facing everyone rather than the TV. The show had barely started, and David began mimicking an act that Red Skelton had done the previous week. He began by taking off one of his shoes and holding up his foot with its white sock. Then David inspected the sock and looked up as if he were surprised. He placed his index finger between his big toe and the next toe and pulled at the sock, then looked up, surprised again, pretending there was a hole in the sock. Next, he held something tightly between his thumb and index finger – an imaginary sewing needle. Then he took his right hand and squeezed his thumb and index finger together tightly and held up... the thread! The family began to giggle as they watched David mimic every detail of the act.

David paused, waiting for the laughter to subside, frozen in his position "holding" the needle and thread. He stuck the imaginary end of the thread in his mouth, pursed his lips around it to wet it, and then began poking at the imaginary needle which he held so close to his nose that his eyes crossed. The family began to laugh hysterically as David poked the needle with the thread over and over, his face scrunching in frustration. Finally, success! He looked up and smiled. Then he took his threaded needle and poked it into one side of the imaginary hole in the toe of his sock. He pulled the thread way up, past his head, until it was taut and yanked gently a couple times to be sure it was as taut as it could get. Then he took another stitch and checked the tautness again, holding the imaginary needle far above his head. Another stitch, then OH! He stuck himself with the needle! David grimaced in pain and grabbed his socked foot and rolled on the floor wincing. The family howled and the girls nearly fell out of their chairs as David continued to stay in character. He regained his composure and picked up the needle once again, sewed three very quick stitches into the sock, wound the thread around in the air three times, stuck the needle through the imaginary loops and made a knot. He bit the imaginary extra thread off with his teeth and suddenly held his arms out wide and smiled. The family cheered and whistled and hooted, "Hurray! Hurray!"

David was a character.

*   *   *

It was 11:42 and Russell couldn't sleep. How could he? He had just been commissioned to make a fishing rod for the president! He rolled over and adjusted his pillow and drew the blanket up tighter around his neck. *One sheep, two sheep, three sheep…*

It was no use. Who decided that counting sheep would make you fall asleep anyway? It was a ridiculous notion. Russell quietly tip-toed out of the room and into the kitchen where he made himself a cup of hot chocolate, then went into the dining room and sat down with a pencil and paper to make himself a few notes - details about the president's fishing rod that he didn't want to forget.

When he finished his hot chocolate, he felt so wide awake that he grabbed his jacket he had left draped over the back of the chair next to the telephone table and put it on over his pajamas. He slipped on his work shoes he had left by the piano. *It's a good thing Edna doesn't mind my things left all over the house,* he thought, otherwise, *she would have to nag real hard to get me to change my bad habits.*

Russell slipped out the front door and drove to the store; he might as well make use of the time if he was going to be awake anyhow.

*   *   *

Russell switched on the lights and stood at the door in his pajamas and coat. He gazed around the store, feeling like a little boy admiring merchandise he only hoped he could one day acquire.

Everything was perfect at the store; it was well organized and sparkling clean. He carried everything any fisherman would ever need or want. Vests, hats, vinyl pants, and boots lined the south wall.

The east wall was the entrance and window display. It looked really nice, and Russell paused to admire it. Edna had just helped him with it the other night. Ken Anderson had given him an old rowboat from a movie set, beat up and worn – the kind that looks like a person had gone fishing in it a million times. It was small and fit perfectly in the front window. He had put a male mannequin, dressed in one of Russ's own plaid flannel shirts along with a fishing vest and hat from his store merchandise, and placed it on the bench seat in the middle. The mannequin, which Russell had named "Stump" – so named because he had no legs – was holding in his hands one of Russell's most popular fishing rods. Above it hung a sign Edna had painted for him, which read: "Wouldn't you rather be fishing?" Russell looked at the display, admiring their work.

On the north wall were his many rods, all lined up and separated by type, and in the middle of his store, in glass display cases, were his lines, flies, reels, and a variety of other fishing paraphernalia. Russell was a humble man, not one to make any to-do about himself, but as he looked around the place, he felt a sense of pride in his accomplishment.

There was a time, well, most of the time, growing up that he would never have imagined himself being successful and having his own store. He only had a 7th grade education. The years during the Great Depression had gotten so bad for his family, that his father had to ask him to drop out of school and go to work instead, to help support the family. Russell had never complained. He loved his family, of course he would help.

He had gotten his first job at a paint supply store. He was just 12 years old and working full time stocking paint cans and sweeping the floors, helping customers find things, and occasionally doing errands for the owner. When he was 17 he became an apprentice to one of the stores' painters and started painting houses. It was decent money, he didn't mind the hard work, and because he was such a perfectionist by nature, he got job after job. In those years, he was one of the lucky ones.

But every weekend, he went fishing. It was his favorite thing in the world to do and he found he had a knack for it. One day, as he watched his fishing rod arch with the weight of a catch, he wondered how they could bend so far and still not break in two. He was a consistent visitor to the local fishing tackle store and the owner liked Russ. He was respectful, quiet, and very curious. Russell would stand beside him and watch silently as a new fishing rod was being turned on the lathe. One day he asked Russell if he would like to try it. Russell was a natural. He made many fishing rods, experimenting with different materials, thicknesses, and lengths. He finally settled on the idea that fiberglass was the best. He bought his own lathe and set it up in the garage. And that's how it all started. He painted houses for another 10 years but made and sold fishing rods from his garage. He finally quit painting and opened his store just before David was born.

And now… now he was going to make a fishing rod for President Eisenhower! Russell chuckled at the thought and looked around his store again. It felt surreal. Out loud he said, "You've done alright Russ Peak. You've done alright."

He turned out the lights and went home.

21

September 4, 1959

RUSSELL WALKED NERVOUSLY to the witness stand. He had never testified in a murder trial before. He wished he were back at the store where he belonged, but Walt was his friend and was in a lot of trouble – of course he would testify for him.

"Raise your right hand please," the bailiff ordered. Russell raised his hand, and the bailiff said the words, "Do you swear to tell the truth, the whole truth, and nothing but the truth, so help you God?"

"I do."

"You may sit down, Mr. Peak." Russell sat down in the hard wooden chair and unbuttoned his suit jacket. He had worn his best church suit to court and a nice brown and silver striped tie. Edna had told him how handsome he looked while they both were getting ready to leave. It was impossible to feel handsome enough to be any more comfortable sitting where he was sitting, about to do what he was about to do. He had never testified in court for anything; the closest he ever got to a trial was jury duty once for a minor incident of breaking and entering.

After a few questions "for the record" the defense attorney turned to Russell and asked, "How long have you known Mr. Borchers?"

"About 10 years."

"Why is Walt Borchers your friend?"

"He's a fine man. He has always been very kind to my wife, my children, and to myself. We enjoy the same kinds of things. I enjoy his sense of humor, and I think he enjoys mine." Russell looked over at Walt sitting at the defense table and thought how very strange it was that they were here, in a courtroom, and he was testifying on Walt's behalf. Walt looked exhausted and sat a little slumped over in his chair, but his eyes were looking hopefully at Russell.

"When you first met Mr. Borchers, he had quite a foul mouth didn't he?" Walt's attorney asked.

"Yes."

"Did you attempt to help him with that?"

"Yes."

"Would you please tell us what you did?"

I made him pay me 50 cents for each swear word he said. I made five dollars the first week." There were light chuckles in the courtroom.

"Does he still have a foul mouth?"

"No."

Walt's attorney came a step closer to Russell and asked, "Do you think someone who took the time to correct a bad habit like swearing would murder someone."

The district attorney quickly called out in a rather loud voice, "Objection, your honor. Calls for speculation."

"Sustained."

Walt's attorney paused as he shuffled through some papers on his desk, then asked Russell, "You believe Mr. Borchers shot his friend Dottie accidentally, is that correct?"

"Yes, that's correct."

"Did Mr. Borchers tell you it was an accident?"

"Yes."

"What did he say?"

"He said it was because of his glass eye; that she had come up to him on his blind side, he was startled, and his gun accidentally went off."

"And you believe him."

"Yes, I do."

"Why do you believe him, Mr. Peak?"

Once again, the district attorney stood and said, "Objection, calls for opinion your honor."

The judge looked at Russell and said, "I'll allow it. You may answer the question Mr. Peak."

Russell shifted in his chair and answered, "Because in my ten years of knowing Walt as a friend, he has always been honest and trustworthy."

"Thank you, Mr. Peak." Walt's attorney sat down and pat Walt on the shoulder.

The district attorney stood, buttoned his suit coat and began his own questions. "Mr. Peak, what did Mr. Borchers tell you about his actions on the night of May 16, 1959?"

"He told me that he had accidentally shot and killed his friend Dottie."

"Is that *all* that he told you Mr. Peak?" the attorney asked suspiciously.

"He asked me what he should do. If that's what you're getting at," Russell said honestly.

"What did you tell him?"

"I told him he should turn himself in to the police and tell them the truth about what had happened."

"Did Mr. Borchers tell you that he and Dottie had quarreled prior to the shooting?"

Russell furrowed his brow slightly and answered honestly, "No."

The district attorney paused for a moment then continued, "Mr. Peak, were you aware that your friend, Walt Borchers, stuffed Ms. Holms' body in his trunk and then drove around for three days with her in there?" He stared straight at Russell as if to say, "Check mate," and waited for Russell to answer.

"I became aware of that after he was arrested."

"As his good friend, do you have any idea why he would do such a thing?"

This time it was Walt's attorney's turn to object, "Objection your Honor, calls for opinion."

"I'll allow it, please answer the question, Mr. Peak."

Russell had already spent many sleepless nights thinking about what Walt had done and didn't have to even bat an eye before answering, "I believe very strongly that Walt was having a nervous breakdown as a result of the shooting, which I still believe was an accident – if that's what your next question was going to be."

"No, that wasn't going to be my next question," the district attorney said, a little annoyed with Russell. "I was going to ask you if you had a degree in psychology Mr. Peak. Do you?"

"No."

"Then how would you know if he was having a so-called nervous breakdown?" he said smugly.

Russell calmly replied, "A person doesn't need a degree in psychology to know when someone's just not right. Do they?"

"I'm asking the questions, Mr. Peak." The attorney fumbled through some papers on the desk for a moment and continued, handing Russell a document. "This is an admission form for Rock Haven Sanitarium, for patient Edna L. Peak. Is that correct Mr. Peak?"

Russell was stunned. Why was he bringing this up? He looked at the admission form and Edna's name on it. His head shot up at

Edna, sitting two benches back from the defense table. She looked lovely in a light pink cotton-lawn dress. Her brown hair was pinned softly away from her face which had turned flush with humiliation. Russell's eyes met hers. He looked back at the district attorney and said, "I don't think that anyone's admission form has anything to do with this trial."

"I didn't ask you what you thought, I asked you if this was an admission form for Edna L. Peak to Rock Haven Sanitarium, dated April 20th, 1952."

"Objection, your honor, what possible relevance does this have to the case?"

The district attorney quickly jumped in, "Your honor, if you will bare with me, I will connect this line of questioning to the case quickly."

The judge looked over the top of his reading glasses and said, "You better," and turning to Russell advised him to go ahead and answer.

Russell looked down at the paper and quietly said, "Yes."

"I'm sorry, I don't think the court could hear your answer. Could you repeat it please."

"Yes," Russell said louder.

"Your wife has had serious mental health issues, correct?"

"Yes, but –"

"Do you trust your wife with your children, Mr. Peak?"

"Yes! Of course I do. What are you getting at?" Russell was downright angry now.

"So, your wife still has self-control enough to *not* kill anyone, even though she has serious mental issues and has been hospitalized for several nervous breakdowns, isn't that right Mr. Peak?"

Russell answered rather quietly as he was feeling confused by the question, "Of course, she would never kill anyone."

"Then why do you think that your friend, Walt Borchers, killed an innocent woman, stuffed her body in his car, and then drove around for three days? Is he just crazier than your wife?"

Russell held his lips together tightly. His face turned red. He looked at Edna who was wiping her eyes with her lace hankie. This was outrageous.

The attorney continued, "In fact, he wasn't crazy at all, he was angry. He was so full of rage that he killed as a result of it, and then tried to cover his crime by stuffing the victim in his trunk while he tried to figure out how to get away with it, isn't that right Mr. Peak?"

Walt's attorney jumped from his seat and yelled out angrily, "OBJECTION, your honor! Leading the witness!"

"I'll withdraw the question," the district attorney said smugly, knowing he had already done what he had set out to do. He walked back over to the prosecutor's table and calmly asked Russell another question. "You're a loyal person, aren't you Mr. Peak? You are fiercely loyal to your wife; I admire that quality." The district attorney used a soft voice, letting the jury see that he wasn't completely insensitive. Russell was quiet and he continued, "But loyalty cannot get in the way of justice. Can it Mr. Peak?"

The district attorney let his final words hang in the air and without asking Russell to actually answer his question, said, "I have no further questions for this witness, your honor," and he sat down at the table, unbuttoned his suit jacket and leaned back in his chair.

Russell felt red in the face. He looked at Edna who was trying to smile at him. Walt sat at the defense table with his head in his hands and his elbows propped up on the table. Russell wasn't sure what he was supposed to do. He wanted to run out of the courtroom with Edna at his side and pretend like the whole thing never happened. His heart was thumping in his chest when Walt's attorney stood and asked the judge if he could re-direct.

"I know this is painful, Mr. Peak, but I need to ask a few more questions." He spoke softly, sensitively, and came around the front of the defense table toward the witness box. "Because of your wife's nervous breakdowns, you *do* have *experience* with this type of mental illness, even though as my distinguished colleague has pointed out, you do not have a degree in psychology, correct?"

"I do have some experience with nervous breakdowns, yes," Russell quietly said.

"Using your own personal experience as a guide, why did you feel Mr. Borchers was suffering a nervous breakdown when he placed Ms. Holms' body in the car?"

Russell expected the district attorney to object, but when he didn't, Russell answered the question. "He had had many difficult and stressful things happen in his life just prior to meeting Dottie and I think the accidental shooting pushed him over the edge, mentally. His mind wasn't quite capable of making good decisions." Russell paused in his testimony and looked sympathetically at Walt. "So, he made a very bad decision," he concluded, looking down at the floor.

"Thank you, Mr. Peak."

Russell stood and walked through the courtroom to the bench where Edna was sitting. He sat down next to her, took her hands from her lap and tenderly held them, then whispered in her ear, "Would you like to go now dear?"

Edna smiled a tear-stained smile and bravely said, "I'm alright darling. I really would like to stay – for Walt's sake."

*   *   *

The trial lasted two weeks. Walt Borchers was found guilty of second-degree murder. But the judge, very unexpectedly, overturned the jury verdict to involuntary manslaughter. Walt was sentenced to serve two years in prison.

One day, after Walt had been in prison for a few months, Russell decided to call the judge to thank him for what he had done.

"Yes, I remember the trial of Mr. Borchers, and of course I

remember *you* Mr. Peak." Judge Stimpson chuckled lightly as he continued, "During the whole trial I kept wishing I could talk to you about your fishing rods. I wanted to visit your store, but of course that was out of the question. Now that the trial is over, I plan on finding the time to stop in."

"You're a fisherman, then?" Russell asked, quite surprised. He kept picturing the judge, in his black robe, knee-deep in a river, casting his rod. It was silly, but that was how his mind pictured it.

"Well, I love to fish, but I'm nothing like the master I've heard *you* are Mr. Peak!"

"Why, thank you, your honor. I'll look forward to seeing you in my store sometime soon. I'll show you a few casting tricks."

"Well, that would be just grand. Now, what can I do for you?"

Russell took one moment to try and clear his mind of fishing and remember what he had called the judge for in the first place. "I was calling to thank you for what you did for Walt in overturning the jury verdict."

There was a pause on the other end of the line. The judge finally said, "No one has ever called to thank me for anything before. I want you to know, Mr. Peak, that it was based on your testimony and strength of character that I decided to overturn the jury verdict at the conclusion of the trial."

"Well... I..." Russell really didn't know what to say. "Thank you, your honor. Thank you very much." Russell hung up the phone and sat for a moment in the chair next to the telephone table. Everything about the phone call had been so unexpected. He pictured the judge fishing in his black robe again and chuckled.

*   *   *

Several years later, when the murder trial had become only a memory, Cherie was on her way to visit her mother and as she approached her father's shop on Allen Avenue, she became concerned because of police cars and emergency vehicles all gathered at the corner, with police tape blocking the entrance to her father's store as well as the drugstore adjoining it on the corner. There on the sidewalk, directly in front of the door to the shop, was a body, covered with a white cloth. Cherie felt as if her heart was going to thump right out of her chest, and she felt sick to her stomach. She felt like rushing to the body and lifting the sheet to look but knew she wouldn't want to see her father like that if it was him. Instead, she quickly drove around to the back parking lot and rushed to the store's back entrance. Finding the door locked, she pounded on the door, shouting for her father, but there was no answer. Cherie was panicked. *Oh dear God, please don't let that be him on the sidewalk*, she silently prayed.

Cherie drove home as quickly as traffic would let her, hoping and praying that she would find him safe and sound. As she rushed through the front door, she immediately saw her mother and father sitting at the dining room table talking and eating sandwiches. She rushed up to her father and tearfully hugged him with all her might. "Dad, oh my gosh you're alive! Thank God!" Cherie squeezed him harder, "I love you so much."

Russell had explained what happened to Edna when he got home and explained it again to Cherie. "I had decided today that I would go home for lunch instead of staying at the store and I was going to go out the front door. As I reached for the front door handle, I remembered that I wanted to take some new feathers home with me to show your mother and get her opinion about them, so I turned to go back and get them. No sooner had I let go of the front door handle and turned around, when I heard several gunshots. I turned and saw a man fall to the ground." Russell gazed at the floor and shook his head. Looking back up at Cherie and Edna he said, "I stood there by the front door utterly stunned. I told the police who questioned me that I was completely unaware of the ruckus, which was an attempted robbery happening next door at the drugstore. Apparently, the man who was shot was someone who got caught in the crossfire. Poor fellow."

"Oh my heavens Dad, that could have been you. So easily it could have been you."

22

November 1961

BOWLING. DAVID LOVED bowling. And amazingly, he was good at it. Mrs. Keith's little school of five students had grown to 16 students and was held in a rented office space. Not all of them were mongoloids like David but had a variety of other handicaps which prevented them from being able to go to public schools. A few months ago, Mrs. Keith and the two assistants whom she had hired, decided to take all the "kids" to the bowling alley. They were always called "the kids" even though a few of them were in their 20's. David was almost 13.

It took David at least 15 minutes to find a ball he liked and that his chubby, short fingers would fit into. Tom, one of the assistants, kept telling him, "This one's perfect David, let's bowl now." But David kept saying, "I no like ith." He looked at nearly every single ball in the place. But finally, he found one his fingers fit into perfectly and it was *red!* David's favorite color.

After a little instruction from Tom, David stood, staring down the lane at the bowling pins, holding his ball up to his chest, ready to go. He stared at the pins. He stood. He stared. Finally, Tom walked up to him and said, "David, are you gonna bowl, or are you gonna stand there?"

"I'm goon bowl," David said as if it was a stupid question.

"O.K. Then get to it little man!"

"O.K. O.K.," David said, annoyed.

Tom sat back down and everyone waited, staring at David. Slowly he walked forward, lifted the ball up slightly, swung it back, then forward, and let it go! He froze in his ending position – right arm up over his head, bent at the waist, and with his right leg lifted up in the air behind him. He stayed frozen until the crash of the pins. A strike! There was a whoop of screaming and hollering from the bench. Tom ran to David, who was just standing at the fault line, and shook his shoulders. "You're unbelievable little man!" David didn't seem to know what all the cheering was for.

"I did ith?" David asked.

"Yeah, you did it! Look! Look, David." Tom turned David around and pointed to the end of the lane at the fallen pins being pushed off the deck by the pinsetter machine. "You got 'em all down! You did it!"

"I did ith!" David smiled his huge smile, so big his eyes almost disappeared. "I did ith!"

Everyone took a turn. Everyone had fun but most of the other kids got gutter balls. It was David's turn again. He picked up his red ball and stood with it to his chest. He stood, he stared. Just when everyone thought he was never going to go, he stepped forward. He lifted the ball up slightly, swung it back, then forward, and let it go. He froze in his ending position: right arm up over his head, bent at the waist, right leg up in the air – exactly the same as the last time in every detail. Except the strike. He knocked down 9 pins. Everyone cheered. David stared at the solitary pin standing and didn't move. Tom finally went to his side, and putting his hand on David's shoulder said, "David, you did great. Twice in a row!"

David pointed to the pin and said, "Look." He looked at Tom with sad eyes.

"No, no David, that's O.K. One pin is nothing! You get another turn. You can still try to get that last one down too! Here." Tom took David's red ball which had just emerged from the pinsetter and handed it to him. "Go again. Look at the pin and don't take your eye off the pin. Try and get it down, but it's O.K. if you don't. You're doing great no matter what. Just have fun!" Tom patted David on the back and sat back down.

David stood with his ball to his chest. Same exact procedure. Whack! He did it! Tom jumped out of his seat and ran to David. He picked him right up out of his frozen position and swung him around yelling, "You did it David!"

The manager of the bowling alley had noticed the ruckus and halfway through the game came over to the group and watched, saying nothing. He just stared at David. Tom had noticed him standing there, approached him and asked if everything was alright. The manager said, "What's wrong with that boy?" pointing to David.

"Does it matter?" Tom said, irritated by the question.

"No, of course not." The manager said, embarrassed. "It's just unusual. I… I mean, he… he's a good bowler. I don't recall seeing him here before."

"That's because this is the first time he's ever bowled." Tom felt in awe of David too. "It's the darndest thing, isn't it? If I wasn't seeing it with my own eyes, I wouldn't believe it either."

*　　*　　*

"How did you like bowling, Davie dear?" Edna asked as David got into the front seat of the car outside the entrance to his school.

"I like bowling. I like bowling." He smiled at her. "I win!"

"You won?"

"Yeth. Tom say I won!"

"Well, for goodness sake!" Edna patted his leg and smiled broadly at him.

David turned from Edna and spoke to the empty back seat, "I won Sally! Arn you proud of me?" He smiled for awhile and made funny, googly faces at the back seat.

A couple months later for his 13th birthday, Edna and Russell gave David his very own bowling ball, red of course, a ball bag, and a bowling glove – which David insisted he needed. Several years later David started bowling in tournaments. He won over and over again.

David was a bowling champion.

23

January 1, 1965

THE FAMILY GATHERED in the living room for a special prayer. Kneeling on the carpet in a circle and taking each other's hands, Russell was the voice for them all, "Please, please, our loving and gracious Father in Heaven, please bring our beloved David back to us safely. Let those around him reach out to him and help him." There was a pause in his words as he tried to compose himself. His voice cracked as he continued, "We ask most humbly for his protection and safekeeping. Please bring him back to us."

The day before had been such a carefree, festive day. Ginny and her husband, Bob, and their little boy, Steven, had arrived all the way from Washington D.C., where Bob was stationed as an officer in the Marine Corps. They had given Edna and Russell their Christmas present which was the announcement of another expected baby the next July. Deanna and her husband couldn't come as Deanna was expecting her first baby to arrive any day. Half a dozen of Edna and Russell's friends had come and Walt Borchers and his new wife, Maria, had come too. The little house in Pasadena was full!

Edna had prepared some finger foods that remained on the table all day for everyone to help themselves: olives, pickles, cheese and crackers, different types of sliced salami, nuts of every kind, oranges, grapes, and several boxes of See's Chocolates. The white lace tablecloth had been pressed and branches from the kumquat tree had been snipped and arranged by Ginny in a blue vase. Cherie had made punch the night before and froze some sliced fruit in little rings which floated about in the punchbowl.

Russell had taken two buckets and a board that stretched between them up to the curbside on Colorado Blvd. Nothing was more fun than spending New Year's Eve sleeping on the street to save a place to watch the Rose Parade on New Year's Day and the family made the effort every year. Their home was just one block south of the parade route and everyone could come and go all night as they pleased. Some slept on the street and some slept at the house. Hot chocolate brewed on the stove all night long and Edna made doughnuts by the dozens. There was noise and music and laughter until around 3am when most folks were too tired to keep up the buzz and began to nod off to sleep in their sleeping bags.

There were huge grandstands erected behind the sidewalks in empty lots to accommodate the thousands of people who arrived on buses to watch the parade. After the parade they returned to their buses and were taken to destinations all over southern California. A few of the buses took people to the Rose Bowl for the football game and some buses took people to Anaheim and dropped them off at Disney Land. The streets were always pure mayhem immediately following the last float, with people scattering everywhere, trying to push their way through the crowd and get to wherever they were going. It was always a struggle for the family to gather up all their things and contend with the crowds. But once they were through the worst part of it and on the sidewalk headed home on Berkeley Avenue, it was an easy walk back to the bustling little house.

That particular New Years' morning, the weather was stunning – the sky was a brilliant blue with white, billowy clouds overhead. David had slept at the house as he always did and the next morning, he was ready to go up the street at exactly 8am to the parade route. He had on his brand new brown quilted jacket he had gotten for Christmas and a baseball cap that Ginny and Bob had given him the day before. No one else was ready to go quite that soon, so Edna let him go by himself. He had gone back and forth the previous evening several times by himself, so Edna felt confident he would be fine.

But when Edna, Ginny, Steven, Walt and Maria reached their saved spots about 20 minutes later, David was nowhere to be found. Russell immediately ran to one of the many police officers on duty for the parade and gave them a description of David. He tried to help them understand that David was a mongoloid and didn't understand many things, nor could he speak very clearly, even though he was almost 16 years old. Then he ran back down to the house to await word from the police, while everyone else waited and searched for him on the parade route.

An hour later the phone rang. The police had found David. He had wandered off to Holliston Avenue where they found him sitting on a bench outside a gas station, happily eating a candy bar that someone David kept saying was a "new friend" had purchased for him from one of the vending machines.

"David, why in heaven's name did you wander off like that?" Russell asked as they walked the seven blocks back to their spot along Colorado Blvd.

"Sally wahthed to go."

"David Russell Peak, don't you blame this on Sally!" Russell was trying very hard not to be angry with David, but he didn't have patience after such a scare.

"Sally wahthed to go," David adamantly repeated.

"Then you should have told her 'NO'!" Russell was forced into pretending Sally was real.

David paused, and said meekly and unconvincingly, "I did Fathuh."

"Oh... David. Just... just don't ever do that again! O.K.?"

Under his breath David whispered, "Sally wahthed to go," but then said, somewhat begrudgingly, "O.K. Fahthuh."

Russell was silent in his frustration for a moment. Then jokingly said, "Next time tell Sally she'll get a spanking if she wanders off with you again."

David didn't say anything until they reached the rest of the group at their spot on the parade route. Edna ran to him and hugged him, and David cried and said, "I sorry Muthuh."

Russell rolled his eyes, but laughed to himself, *fine, apologize immediately to your mother, but make excuses to me! Stubborn David!*

*   *   *

The parade was thoroughly enjoyed by the family, especially in light of the terrible scare they had endured that morning. After the last float went by everyone quickly stood and began gathering the buckets, lawn chairs, sleeping bags, blankets, and thermoses. Edna turned to David and asked him to please help her carry the buckets back to the house. She turned from him to make sure they had picked up all their belongings. That was the last she saw David.

*   *   *

After Russell finished the family prayer, they were all trying to comfort each other and think positively when there was a loud knock on the front door. The police had come to the house to take a description of David.

120

One officer, after writing everything down, paused and then said, "This sounds just like a boy that went missing just this morning."

"It *is* the same boy," Russell said, his bright blue eyes now filled with worry.

The officer looked at him for a moment, then said, "Do you mean to tell me he's gone missing twice in the same day?" When no one offered a reply, he simply asked, "Do you have any idea where you think he may have gone *this* time?"

"No. We already looked for him on Holliston Avenue where he was found this morning." Russell tried to think and dug his hands deep into his pants' pockets. He looked up, his eyes wide, and said, "I sure hope he didn't get on one of those tour buses. He loves to ride the bus."

Edna came to his side and looked at him with pleading in her face, "Oh Russell, you don't think he would ever actually get on one of those buses, do you?"

"I don't know, dear. I sure hope not."

The police continued to question everyone, but Russell left the group and went to the telephone, calling as many bus lines as he could think of. He gave them a description of David but with each call he became more discouraged. He turned to Edna and said, "They all tell me the same thing – that there are hundreds of people on those buses, going to different destinations, making different stops, and it will be nearly impossible to find him, even if he *was* on one of the buses." Russell took a deep breath and added, "They did say, however, that they would try to alert as many drivers as they could with David's description."

Russell turned back to the telephone and called Ken Anderson and told him that David was missing. He told him there was a possibility he could have gotten on a bus headed for Disney Land. Ken called the park, gave them David's description and had an alert put out for him. Ken assured Russell that if David ended up at Disney Land, they would find him.

The family all tried to have faith that everything would turn out alright but couldn't help but worry themselves sick. No one touched a bite of food and the mood was somber. Several of their good friends from church came to the house to offer comfort and support and their prayers. Deanna had even come, as uncomfortable in her pregnancy as she was.

By 9:00 that evening the police put David's description on teletype. The family waited. Edna tried to be brave, but she had to go into her room several times and weep.

At 9:35 that evening a yellow taxicab pulled up at the curb outside the house. Deanna and Cherie, who were sitting together on the couch, noticed the taxicab and wondered what it was doing arriving at their house. Suddenly, Cherie sprang to her feet shouting, "IT'S DAVID! IT'S DAVID!" as she ran to the door. David was just getting out of the door of the cab as he was greeted by a mob of hugs and kisses. His new jacket was missing, but other than that he seemed to be cheerful and unruffled. The cab driver stood politely at the trunk of his cab and smiled as he watched the happy reunion. Edna and Russell alternated between hugging David, crying, and hugging each other.

When they had quieted down sufficiently, Russell approached the driver and asked him if he would come in for a moment and tell them how it was that he had brought David to them and have something to drink and eat.

The cab driver sat in the wingback chair, a plate of food on his lap and a drink of hot chocolate on the side table next to him, while everyone sat around him eager to find out what he knew. "I first seen your boy at the corner of sixth and Grand, near the Savoy Hotel in downtown Los Angeles. He looked lost, so I asked him if he needed help. He said the funniest thing!" The cab driver took a big bite of his sandwich and chewed while the family sat with anticipation. "He said, 'Man, please take me home!' So, I helped him into my cab – his mind was real set on sitting in the front seat – then I asked him where he lived." He said, 'Pasadena' so that's where I headed."

The family was already astonished. The stranger sitting in their living room had their undivided attention. He continued, "When I got to the Pasadena exits, I asked him if he knew which one to take. He didn't answer me at first, so I slowed down, and he finally pointed to the Allen Avenue exit and said, 'That one.' I turned off the freeway and went along real slow and he pointed to which turns to take until a few moments ago when he said, 'That's my house.' So, I stopped."

Edna, Ginny and Deanna were crying with relief. Russell asked how much the fare was and the driver answered that he didn't want anything for the fare. Russell insisted that they pay for the long ride. The cab driver shrugged his shoulders and said, "I did it 'cause I wanted to help him out. We all gotta just help each other sometimes, so you don't gotta pay me mister."

They thanked him profusely for bringing David safely home to them and walked him back out to his taxicab. Edna handed him a sack with goodies she had gathered from the table of food and everyone waved goodbye to him as he drove away.

Back inside the house, Edna made David a peanut butter and mayonnaise sandwich, just the way he liked it – thin peanut butter, thick mayo. He had wandered around all day with only six cents in his wallet – a new one he had gotten from his best friend, Bobby Durfee, for Christmas. How unfortunate that Edna had not thought to put identification in the wallet! David poked at his meal and only nibbled on it.

"Aren't you hungry darling?" Edna asked, surprised he wasn't devouring his favorite sandwich in the whole world.

"Lady bawth hambuhguh," David said.

"A lady bought you a hamburger?" Edna asked?

"Yeth."

"David, where did you go today?" Everyone in the room was listening, hoping to understand his words enough to figure out the mystery of where exactly he had spent New Year's Day.

"Buth."

"You rode a bus somewhere?" Russell asked.

"Yeth."

"Where did the bus take you?"

"To Butheth."

"To another bus?"

"Yeth."

"Then where did that bus go?" Ginny asked as the family sat on the edge of their seats to hear the remarkable tale.

"Game."

"Game? You played a game?"

David stood up from the table and put his arms straight up in the air and yelled "TUTHDOWN!" Then he pretended to limp and walked over to the couch and sat down, then elevated his "injured" foot in the air. It was like a game of charades.

"David, did you go to a football game today?"

"Yeth."

The family laughed, cheered, and gasped. David had gone to the Rose Bowl game! It was Michigan vs. Oregon. Here *they* had all missed watching the game on television on account of David being... AT the game!

"Did the lady buy you the hamburger at the game?"

"Yeth."

"My oh my David, how did you manage to get someone to buy you a hamburger?"

"I sayth, 'I hungry'!" David smiled.

"You told a lady at the Rose Bowl game that you were hungry."

"Yeth."

Edna giggled and asked, "After the game ended where did you go?"

"Buth."

"You got on another bus?"

"Yeth. Hotel. Up, down, up, down. Hotel."

Edna repeated his words to herself, stumped. Everyone tried to figure out what he meant. David added more to his account, "Buthuns. Puth buthuns."

"Pushed button!" Deanna exclaimed.

"Yeth!" David was having fun at this game.

"A hotel elevator! Did you ride a hotel elevator up and down, David?" asked Deanna.

The charades game was suddenly interrupted by the telephone ringing. Ginny was closest and picked up the receiver. "Hello, Peak residence." Pause. "Oh, I see." Pause. "Yes, he was found and is here, safe and sound." Long pause. "Thank you so much for calling. We appreciate it very much." Ginny hung up and related the conversation to the curious family and friends all gathered in the living room. "That was a driver from one of the bus lines. He said he heard David's description over the radio and recalled that earlier he had seen a boy fitting David's description getting onto another bus headed for downtown Los Angeles. He called his manager who had our phone number from Dad's earlier calls to the bus lines and so he was calling to pass along the information. He was very happy to know that David is home safe.

The group sighed and expressed gratitude for the driver's call as Ginny sat back down next to Bob.

Returning to David's story, Bob asked David, "Did you have fun riding the elevator and pushing all the buttons, David?"

"Yeth, Bob!" David again smiled his huge, silly grin.

Bob put the final pieces of the puzzle together and said, 'It must have been after he left the hotel that the cab driver saw him and picked him up." Everyone sat in stunned silence, letting the extraordinary events of the day sink into their minds.

Russell finally broke the silence and said, "God has certainly answered our prayers! And what a day Davie had! He took three buses, played in a fancy hotel, had a hamburger, and saw the Rose Bowl football game. All on SIX CENTS!"

*　　*　　*

The next day the phone rang. It was Deanna's husband, Gary, calling to inform the family that she had given birth during the night to a baby boy they had named James Russell.

24

July 1965

THE WEEK AFTER the Peaks came home from their summer camping trip in Montana, the phone rang. It was their family doctor who wanted to meet with Edna and Russell in his office the next day. "I have something to tell you of great importance to you, and indeed to many families like you," he had said without being willing to tell them any details. Russell and Edna were very curious about what he could possibly need to meet with them about.

The next day they arrived at Dr. Peterson's office and were greeted enthusiastically and asked to take seats at his desk. The office was simple and Dr. Peterson's file cabinet was crowded with patient files stacked high enough that Edna thought they might just topple over any minute. He had a large, dark walnut desk that, in contrast to the file cabinet, was clear of clutter with the exception of a few items placed purposefully at the corners, and a large book sitting open in the center.

Dr. Peterson sat across from Edna and Russell and began, "Last week I attended a large medical conference. Among the many lectures was one of particular interest." He looked at both of them with a large grin on his face. "The lecture was given by a group of geneticists who had been working on understanding mongolism for the past 15 years and a few years ago, they finally discovered the cause." He pushed the large book sitting on his desk across to Edna and Russell and continued, "They discovered that in all the DNA test cases they were studying, there was an extra chromosome, and in every single case it was on the 21st chromosome." He pointed to an illustration in the book. "All chromosomes have a match, making a perfect pair, but with children like David, they have three instead of two, on chromosome number 21. They gave the condition the medical term of 'Trisomy 21'." He paused and waited as Edna and Russell looked at the picture in the book.

Edna remembered a biology class she had taken in college that had discussed chromosomes and genetics, but it had been a long time and her memory of it was foggy, but this seemed pretty simple to understand. She glanced at Russell, who was still looking at the funny little x's on the page, all paired up with a match, except for the one marked with a "21" underneath the trio. She didn't know if he understood it all but didn't want to embarrass him by asking. Much to her relief, Russell looked up and said, "Looks like chromosome 21 is a popular little fellow in special people like David."

Dr. Peterson smiled, "That's a good way to put it!" then leaned back in his chair and added, "The geneticists also had discussed the fact that the term 'mongoloid idiocy' – the official term used, is racist and, well, unkind. They have officially adopted a new term which they just announced at the conference last week. The new name is 'Down Syndrome.'"

* * *

That evening Edna and Russell sat down in the living room with Deanna and Cherie. They had talked it over and decided it would be a good thing to explain what they had learned about David's condition with them. All three of the girls were married now and Deanna and Cherie still lived close by. Ginny and Bob still lived in Washington D.C. and were expecting their second child any day now, so Edna and Russell would wait to tell them about David when they got the call about the new baby.

They were especially happy with the new name: *Down Syndrome*. They liked it. For some reason they had never liked having to call David "a mongoloid," as if he were from some other planet. Dr. Peterson said that eventually, people would become so familiar with the term that it would become easier and easier for people to understand why David was the way he was. It was also such a relief for Edna to find out that *she* had not done anything to cause David's condition.

"Mother and Dad, if this is genetic, does that mean that we could have a baby with Down Syndrome?" asked Deanna, who was holding 6-month-old baby Jimmy on her lap.

"Dr. Peterson said that so far, they feel it is purely a random occurrence, and that it is not inherited. So, in other words, no – it doesn't mean you or Cherie or Ginny will have a baby with Down Syndrome. But they are still studying that part of things."

"This means David will always have this, his whole life, right?" asked Cherie.

"Yes, that's right dear."

"Why did they name it *Down Syndrome*? Why not *Up Syndrome*?" joked Deanna.

Edna began to explain, "Apparently, in the late 1800's, a man named John Langdon Down first made the observation that there were similarities in some individuals: the mental disabilities, the short fingers, the almond shaped eyes and other things. He named the people 'mongoloids' after their resemblance to people of the Mongolian race. Earlier this year, the group of scientists who were studying the disorder felt it needed a new name and they figured they should name it after Mr. Down who first characterized its features."

"So, when people ask us what's wrong with David, we just tell them he has Down Syndrome, right?" asked Cherie.

"That's exactly right. Dr. Peterson said that eventually people will become familiar with the term." As an after-thought Edna continued, "He also said that more people are keeping babies like Davie instead of putting them away in an institution and so people will start to recognize the condition more and more. And now with its new name, and all the understanding about it and what causes it, Dr. Peterson feels that eventually, people with Down Syndrome will be more accepted in society."

*   *   *

Two weeks later the phone rang. It was Bob and Ginny calling from Washington D.C.

"Just thought you'd like to know you have a granddaughter! We named her Jill."

"Oh! How delightful!" Edna exclaimed excitedly. She had secretly hoped it would be a girl. Now Edna and Russell were proud grandparents of two boys and one girl.

"Daddy and I have some rather exciting news to tell you about too!"

25

May 1968

D AVIE, WILL YOU please take off your new yellow shirt and put on one of your plain white t-shirts?" Edna asked sweetly as she came into his room carrying a tray holding his breakfast.

"No, I wonth!" David announced.

"David darling, don't speak to your mother that way. Please just put on the white shirt. I will take you and Bobby bowling later this afternoon after I come home from the library."

"I wonth do ith!" Go out!" David was unusually upset.

"I don't want you to get egg all over your new shirt. Ginny gave that one to you for your birthday. Don't you want to keep it nice?"

David just stared at Edna and rocked back and forth, sitting on the edge of his bed. He looked angry and began to clack his teeth – a habit that had never gone away. Edna stared back at him as he rocked and clacked. It didn't feel worth the strain, so she put the tray down on the bed next to him and walked out toward the kitchen. She could hear him angrily mumbling to himself, "Davith, I have 1 shuth, 2 shuth, 3 shuth, I got 5 shuths."

He must be thinking that he has so many other shirts, why am I making a big fuss about the yellow one? Edna thought, trying to make sense of what he was saying.

She ate her breakfast by herself in the kitchen and worked on the crossword puzzle in the newspaper, part of her daily routine. After about 20 minutes, David came in with his dirty dishes, put them in the sink and began to wash them, as well as the dishes from Edna's breakfast. He had on a white t-shirt with yellow egg yolk dripped down the front.

"David, I'm sorry about the shirt. Thank you for putting on your white one. You're a good boy." Edna smiled at him, walked over to him and gave him a kiss on his forehead.

David turned and gave her the evil-eye, something he had done and perfected many years previously, but quickly broke out in a huge smile, with his tongue protruding between his lips the way his larger-than-life smile always looked and said, "I gooth boy! I gooth boy."

Edna watched him as he washed, dried, and put away all of the dishes. He took a rag and wiped the counters, getting every single tiny drip, crumb, or sticky spot. Then he folded the wet rag carefully in half, then in half again, then again, and one more time until the rag was folded into the tiniest square he could get it. Then, satisfied that the rag was sufficiently folded, he set it down on the counter next to the sink. He stood at the counter for a few more minutes, patting the tiny square of dish rag, then pausing, then patting. Pat, pause. Pat, pause. David's daily routine.

Edna thought about how helpful David was. He did so many things around the house that made her life easier, even when it wasn't done as perfectly as he did the dishes. One day she had asked him to take everything off his bed and change it, so he did. He took everything off, turned them around, and put them back on. She had to laugh! He had done exactly what she had asked. David also routinely helped with the laundry and one day he had come up to

Edna and said, "Clozin" which she didn't understand and asked him several times to repeat it. He had finally become exasperated, took a deep breath, and very slowly and plainly said, "CLOTHES IN." Edna felt badly for not understanding that "Clozin" was "Clothes in," because he always brought the clothes in from the line in the backyard, folded everything, and put everything away where it belonged.

On another occasion Edna was sitting in her chair watching TV when David, who was sitting on the floor, noticed her arms and said, pointing to her left arm, "That one ith alright," and pointing to her right arm said, "That one ith bad." She had scratched it up that afternoon while cutting shrubbery and it had become a blotchy, bloody mess. That night he had helped her make dinner, scrubbed the potatoes, mixed the ingredients for meat loaf, and put everything in the oven for her. When she had given him a kiss on the forehead, telling him that she loved him a LOT, she heard him mumbling as he walked away, "That was a poor kisth," but then laughing about it.

Edna stood from her perch on the kitchen stool and said, "Davie dear, if you want or need anything while I'm gone today, just go next door and ask Mrs. White to call Ginny." It was like telling a child not to put a bean in his nose...

*   *   *

When Edna returned home several hours later, David was not there. She found two empty TV dinner trays on the floor of David's room and his record player was still turned on. There was no evidence that Ginny had been there at all and no note on the door from the Whites. So, she went across the street to Greg Sage's house where David sometimes played. He wasn't there. Next she went down the street to Hamilton Elementary School, hoping to find him playing on the swings. He wasn't there either. Panic began to settle in and Edna ran back to the house. She tried to call Russell, but he had been at a manufacturing company all day cutting some fiberglass and apparently had still not returned to the store. She ran next door to the White's and asked if they had seen Davie at all that day.

"Yes, he came over a few hours ago and acted as if he were sick. We tried to call Russ at his store, but there was no answer."

Edna's face began to flush. Why had she been so foolish? She had never before told David to go to the White's house, he must have thought she had ordered him to go and was trying to please her. But sick? He had obviously been well enough to gobble down not one, but two TV dinners. He must have been acting. He was a professional, highly paid, famous actor after all.

Apologetically Edna explained, "I told him to come here if he needed anything, but I forgot to inform *you* that I had given him those instructions." Edna glanced back toward the house, hoping perhaps to see David in the yard or on the porch. "He was supposed to tell you to phone Ginny. She and Bob have moved back from Washington D.C."

"Well, when we couldn't reach Russ, we phoned Deanna. She quickly came and took David to her house."

Edna thanked her and rushed home to call Deanna.

"Mother, didn't you see the note I left for you?"

"Well, if I had seen a note, I wouldn't have needed to panic," Edna said with very uncharacteristic anger.

Deanna was hurt and silent for a moment, then rather quietly said, "I'm sorry Mother. I left it on the dining room table."

Edna turned around and looked at the table, still holding the telephone receiver in her hand. She saw a note, in Deanna's handwriting, sitting on top of a stack of newspapers. Edna felt ashamed of herself and her behavior. "Oh Deanna, darling, I'm so sorry. It's right here on the table. I didn't see it. Please forgive me for snapping at you. I would hate to hurt your feelings."

"It's alright Mother, all's well that ends well. David is here safe and sound and he's eating a giant peanut butter and mayo sandwich he fixed for himself."

"He is? Mrs. White said David was acting ill."

Deanna laughed. "Sick! HA! David, I assure you Mother, is feeling perfectly fine. *Acting* is right!"

∗   ∗   ∗

Edna went to bed early that night feeling fatigued and a bit depressed. How could she have been so careless? She felt like a bad mother. She stared at the ceiling and let her mind go wild, imagining all sorts of horrible things that could have happened to David as a direct result of her carelessness. But the fact was, that everything had turned out fine. Russell just chuckled at her account of the day's mishap. He certainly didn't blame her or accuse her of being careless. As a matter-of-fact she heard him in David's room that evening, lecturing David that he was old enough to be a little more responsible.

David said with questioning eyes, "Rebonthbabuhl?"

"Re-spon-si-ble. David. Responsible."

"REEEETH-PON-DA-BA-BLE," David tried again.

Russell caught himself. He could see that David was getting frustrated trying to pronounce a difficult word and please his Dad. How could David understand? He was 19 years old, chronologically, but really, he was about 4 or 5 years old mentally. He didn't need to be more responsible. He was a good boy.

26

May 1968

THREE DAYS AFTER Russell's talk with David about being more, "REETH-PON-DA-BA-BLE," David was in his room, listening to his records and no doubt kissing the pretty face of a blond off one of the record covers. Edna thought it was disgusting the first time she came into his room and found him sitting on the edge of his bed with a record cover pressed to his face. He startled when she walked in and quickly put the record cover down. When she looked at it, lying on the bed, she noticed that the mouth of the blond girl printed on the cover was almost completely worn off. She instinctively said "DAVID! Don't do that! You shouldn't do that."

But later that evening she told Russell about it and he laughed so hard he had tears coming out of his eyes. "Oh Edna, that's the funniest thing I've ever heard! Poor boy. He likes girls! Just like the rest of us men. If he wants to kiss the face off a record cover, who really cares? What's the harm? It's probably the only kissing he'll ever get to do."

During the afternoon, Edna sat in the living room working on a painting. She had recently taken a painting class and was enjoying her newly discovered talent immensely, when David appeared from the hallway. Walking past her towards the door, he calmly said, "Muthuh, there's a fire in my room," and he walked out the front door.

At first Edna didn't believe him. Nevertheless, she put down her painting and went to his room to investigate. As she came closer to his door, which he had shut, she could see flickering light from the crack under the door. Alarmed, she flung the door open. The drapes and his twin bed were ablaze! She ran to the phone and called the fire department. After giving them their address, she quickly ran to get the small fire extinguisher they kept next to the fireplace. Edna did her best, but the fire had become too large and the extinguisher was too small. The smoke was becoming thick, so she scooched down under the choking smoke and joined David out on the front porch.

Within minutes, the fire department arrived. Russell was right behind them and wanted to help. Edna begged him not to – partly because she didn't want him to be endangered and partly because she didn't want him to get in the way. "Fires should be put out by trained professionals," she told him, pleading with him not to go into the house. But he insisted and disappeared into the house anyway.

A small crowd of curious onlookers had gathered outside to watch the commotion. One woman wearing a wig and heavy make-up came up to Edna and spoke to her. At first Edna thought she was just another stranger, but then recognized her as a former neighbor who had moved to the other end of the street into an apartment building. At first, she was very nice, but as they talked, Edna got the impression that the woman was glad their walls and furniture were going to be blackened by the smoke; she seemed so smug about it and Edna wondered if she were jealous of their possessions. *On the other hand,* she thought, *perhaps I am being unnecessarily suspicious. But then again,* Edna let her thoughts continue to flop back and forth, *that wigged woman distinctly gave me a bad feeling.*

No one else talked to Edna, but everyone talked amongst themselves, looking at her, David, and then the house. Edna wondered what they were saying about her. Were they blaming her? Were they thinking cruel things about David and whispering about his handicap?

Her suspicious thoughts were interrupted by the fire chief, Mr. Holmes. "Mrs. Peak, do you think you could try and find out from your son how exactly the fire was started?" Mr. Holmes had very kind, sympathetic blue eyes, and seemed to be very understanding. He knew David from Mrs. Keith's school, which now had over 60 students and was located near the fire station. David had turned in several false alarms at the school so Chief Holmes and five other fire fighters had come to the school and talked with all the kids about what to do in case of a fire.

"David really did exactly what we taught the kids to do, Mrs. Peak. You should be very proud of him. He shut the door, remained calm, reported the fire to an adult, got out of the building and stayed out until it was safe!" Chief Holmes looked over at David who had been staring at his firefighter's uniform in awe. "David's a hero!" he said and stuck his hand out to David to shake it. David looked him square in the eyes and echoed, "Hero. Hero."

*   *   *

Edna never could make sense of anything David said to account for the cause of the fire. One thing was nearly certain – David couldn't have started it. He didn't even know how to strike a match. Mrs. White, from next door, had said that she saw a man run down her driveway that very morning and then she had found several matchbooks on the sidewalk at the end of their driveway later that evening. But who would want to hurt them? Edna tried not to think about it, but occasionally she would let her imagination and paranoia get the best of her and come up with all kinds of wild scenarios of evil men lurking near their home, determined to set it ablaze. Once, she confided to Russell one of her theories. Russell stared back at her with his blue eyes for several moments before finally responding, "I'm sure there must be a..." he searched for just the right words, "more logical explanation." He hadn't searched long enough, apparently. Edna became angry and accused him of accusing her of not being logical. Russell's calm and patient nature won out though, and the fight didn't last very long. He just simply said, "I'm sorry, Dear. You could be right, but I don't think we'll ever know exactly how that fire got started." Edna knew he was right on this fact and dropped the subject. She eventually quit thinking about it all together.

Despite occasionally obsessing over the cause of the fire, everything in the end had worked out just fine. Chief Holmes made it as easy as possible for them in his report to the insurance company – who sent an agent out to the house within two days of the fire to survey the damage. The insurance company, that Edna found to be most helpful, efficient, and polite, paid for all of the necessary repairs. They had to completely re-build David's room and repair plaster from smoke damage in the hall and bathroom. David's furniture, drapes, clothes, record player, and most of his beloved records, including the kissed-off blond, were destroyed.

The first day that the construction workers were there they pulled down the remaining fragments of walls, ceiling, baseboards, and doorjambs. About an hour after they began working, one large, burly man came to Edna holding something wrapped in a half-burned up sheet she recognized as David's extra set she kept in his closet. "Ma'am, I found this at the back of the closet. It's the only thing in there we found that wasn't damaged." He handed the bundle to her and she pulled back the sheet. Gasping, she gazed down at David's lovely violin with his name carved on the back, kept miraculously safe from the fire by a half burned up sheet.

27

August 5, 1968

EDNA NEEDED A vacation, and Russell knew it. The last few years had been full to the brim with major events – some good, some bad, some stressful, some enjoyable. But all of them combined to create strain in Edna's fragile mental well-being. He could see all the signs of another major problem brewing. Russell wanted to help Edna clear her mind and relax, so he decided that this year just the two of them would go to Montana. He made arrangements for David to stay at Bobby Durfee's house for two weeks while he took Edna on vacation.

To pass the hours and hours of driving, the two of them played a game they had enjoyed for years, they had to say a funny quote as fast as they could. The first one to get stumped, or laugh, lost. Russell started, "A closed mouth gathers no foot."

Edna quickly contributed hers, "Cheer up, things could be worse. So, I cheered up and sure enough things got worse."

"Smart is when you believe only half of what you hear. Brilliant is when you know which half." Russell looked at Edna and winked at her.

"There are only two kinds of people: those you like, and those you don't." Edna winked back at Russell.

"Growing old is a matter of mind over matter. If you don't mind – it doesn't matter."

"Bob Newhart is a good actor, so am I."

Russell burst out laughing. "That's not fair! You cheat! You can't quote DAVID!"

"Says who? There is no rule against quoting someone you know. I won."

Russell scoffed and feigned disapproval, "You always win. I can never out-quote you, you read like a maniac." As soon as the word came out of Russell's mouth, he regretted it. He glanced quickly at Edna, but thankfully, she didn't seem to have noticed it. She was still celebrating her victory by smiling and patting her own self on her shoulders.

Russell reached down and picked a chocolate out of the Sees Candy box that was lying open on the seat between them and raised it to Edna's mouth. "Here, a chocolate for the winner!" Edna grinned as he popped the entire chocolate into her mouth.

"Do you remember the first time we met?" Russell asked.

Of course I do. How could I ever forget one of the most important days of my life?" Edna beamed as she picked up a chocolate and put it in Russell's mouth.

"I was a young man trying to eek out a living painting houses," he began as soon as he had swallowed the chocolate. "One day I was carefully painting the trim around a window when I saw in the refection, a beautiful girl strolling out of the house across the street."

"I wasn't strolling. Or beautiful. I was more like traipsing, and dirty," Edna corrected. "I came out in an old work dress with dirt on the front and continued my chore of pulling weeds. But then I noticed the very handsome young man painting the house across the street." Edna took Russell's free hand and gave it a squeeze. "So, I went inside and changed into my new red dress, fixed my hair and *then* came *strolling* out!"

"I only remember the red dress and the strolling part. Not the weed part," Russell said as he squeezed Edna's hand back. "And handsome? I wasn't handsome. I had paint smeared on my face and a pair of old, paint-splattered overalls on. You, on the other hand, were stunning in that red dress. I noticed right off your great legs" Russell said in an overtly flirty way. "I remember you *strolling* through the yard, cutting flowers with a pair of shears. You didn't even notice me." Russell made a sad, frowny face at Edna, who picked up on his hint.

"Didn't notice you? How could I not notice you? *I* was the one trying to get noticed." Edna reached for another chocolate. "Do you know, the entire time I picked those silly flowers I was sneaking glances your way? I was hoping you would fall off your ladder or something, just so I could run to your aid and meet you. Of course, I didn't want you to actually hurt yourself."

"I should have gone across the street and just introduced myself. What a putz I was!" Russell said shaking his head.

"I was indeed terribly disappointed not to meet you that day. I remember going back in the house after you had left and pouting around the place all day. I was a silly girl."

"I was a foolish boy for being so shy."

Edna still, after 33 years, felt flattered and even flirty to hear Russell retell how he felt the first time he saw her. Sometimes, when she pictured that day in her mind, she would feel nervous butterflies in her stomach remembering how handsome he was. She looked over at him, driving, and even through the lines and wrinkles of aging, she could still see him, strong and young, standing on the ladder painting the trim around her neighbor's house. She could so distinctly remember longing to meet him and talk to him.

"Thank goodness for my father. Moving to California turned out to be the best thing he ever did. I hated him for it at first." Edna grew quiet for the moment, regretting that she had ever been so angry at her father.

"And don't forget what good fortune it was to work at Franklin School. That's where you met Clair," Russell added.

"If I hadn't met Clair, I never would have met *you*! Unless, of course, you happened to paint another house just across the street from mine."

Russell shook his head in disbelief, "I'll never forget the moment I walked into Clair's house. She had told me she wanted me to meet a coworker of hers and to come to her house that Friday night for a party. What a shock! It was the girl in the red dress!" Russell looked over at Edna with a broad smile, "Not everyone gets a second chance like that!"

"I remember that moment too. Although, I must admit, I didn't know it was the cute painter from across the street at first. You looked different without the paint on your face. Better! I might add. It was hard not to stare at your blue eyes all night. Your eyes – that's what made me remember who you were. I couldn't believe it was you either. Just goes to show it was providence." Edna laughed as she continued, "I remember all those card tricks you did! Imagine being so impressed by some silly card tricks. But impressed I most certainly was. I don't think I could take my eyes off you all night. I watched you out of the corner of my eye the entire evening."

"You did?" Russell loved hearing this part of their first meeting over and over, even though he had every word of it memorized. He never tired of reminiscing with Edna over their love story. It felt just like yesterday sometimes.

"Of course I did," she indulged him. "You were the most handsome man I had ever seen."

"I was?" Russell asked, basking in the warmth of her compliments.

"Still are," Edna patted his knee and gave it a squeeze.

"You're still the beautiful girl in the red dress to me. You always will be." Russell looked across the seat at his sweetheart. Too bad he had to keep driving. "I do remember the one disappointment of the evening. And it was a pretty big one."

"You mean that you were almost three years younger than me? That one?" Edna said, teasing. She knew which disappointment he meant.

"Oh, ha ha. I mean the one where I found out you had a steady beau."

"Aaaahhh, *that* one," she teased some more.

"I was walking you home from the party, stumbling awkwardly over every word I tried to say to you – I was so nervous. I finally got the nerve to ask if you would go to a movie with me the next evening and… I heard a pop. It was the gunshot to my heart." Russell grasped his chest as if he were feeling the pain. "You nonchalantly said, 'Oh I have a boyfriend.'" Russell made a snorting sound and added, "Minor detail," and looked at Edna to wait for her excuses.

"I know, I know. But *you* got the girl in the end."

"How very true, Mrs. Peak. I'm a lucky man that Lee lived all the way in Minnesota. It's a good thing it's so difficult to go steady with someone halfway across the country. Poor Lee," Russell said mockingly as he took another chocolate and tossed it into his mouth triumphantly.

"Do you remember the Valentine's Day Dance we went to?"

"Yes I do. You wore that beautiful red dress I had first seen you in."

"We had only been seeing each other for a few weeks when we went to that dance. But of course, I knew I was in love with you. And that night you did the cutest thing a boy had ever done for me. Do you remember what it was?"

"Was it the nail polish?"

"You painted tiny red hearts on each of my fingernails and said that's how many times you were going to tell me you loved me that night!"

"Pretty clever, wasn't I?"

"More than clever. Romantic and sweet. It was the first time you told me that you loved me. And then to do it with such style!" Edna said with great flair, waving her arms in the air. "You had me hook, line, and sinker!"

Russell chuckled, "Thanks for using a fishing term. Very clever of *you* my dear!" But there was still one minor detail – Lee."

"That's right. I guess I still had not broken things off with him yet, had I." Edna searched her mind trying to remember the timing of events.

"Nope," Russell said as if he were still hurt. "You didn't break things off with him until after we were engaged!"

"Oh, that's right," Edna looked down at her lap, a little ashamed even all these years later, that she hadn't done things differently. "I waited until Lee came out to California to see me. As it turned out, it would have been more merciful on my part if I had simply done it in a letter. Apparently, he had been planning on asking me to marry him during his visit. Poor Lee," Edna said sincerely. "I remember the moment I broke the news to him that I was engaged to you. He had barely walked in the door with Daddy, who had picked him up at the bus station. Lee leaned down to give me a kiss and I turned my head so that it landed on my cheek and I quickly blurted out that I was engaged. Daddy could have slapped me! He liked Lee so much. He was a college graduate in engineering and Daddy thought he was my equal. Of course, what did Daddy know." Edna squeezed Russell's knee, which she was still resting her hand on. "He hated you at first," Edna laughed. "He thought a college education was everything. You know he threatened to shoot me if I married you."

Russell moaned, "Yes, I know. I'm not crazy about this part of our story."

"He loves you dearly now."

"I know."

"Well… anyway… Lee was heartbroken. He took me canoeing at Westlake Park the next day. I was so conscience stricken when I noticed tears brimming in his eyes as he poured his heart out to me and begged me to reconsider my decision. I felt so sorry for him. Edna imagined poor Lee's heartbroken face with tears streaming down his cheeks. "However, he was a good loser."

"Loser is right!"

"Russell! Be kind."

"Oh Edna, you know Lee and I became very friendly. He was a fine person. Well-liked by everyone, me included. I'm just glad that *I* got the beautiful prize."

Edna smiled over at Russell and said, "I love you Sweetheart Darling."

"I love you, Honey Girl."

Edna thought for a moment before asking, "When did we start calling each other that anyway? And when did we shorten them to S.D. and H.G.?"

"Well, let's see… I think it was just after we got married, wasn't it?"

"Yes, I think you're right. Or was it just before?" There was a quiet intermission as they both thought hard. "I remember you left me a note one day on the table with some flowers… they were in a vase, without any water," Edna giggled. "Yes, it must have been after we were married. I loved that you called me Honey Girl. I've always loved it."

"You looked beautiful on our wedding day. Gosh! I couldn't take my eyes off you. And you were going to be all mine!" Russell looked lovingly over at Edna but noticed a rather serious look cloud her expression.

"Too bad for you, poor thing," she replied as she turned her face to look out the window.

"What do you mean, 'too bad for me?' You are the best thing I ever won in my life."

Edna was somber and somewhat melancholy. "You are much too good to me, Russ Peak."

Russell slowly pulled the car off the highway and onto the shoulder. He turned the engine off and looked very serious as he said, "Now you listen here my little Honey Girl," and he took her face in his hands. "I love you to pieces. I would be miserable if I didn't have you. No one can love *me* like *you* do. Any bad times we have are just part of our journey through life together and I can't stand the thought of making the trip without you. I love you even more because of your determination, and your courage, and your faithfulness – even with your challenges. God gave you those challenges, and you are more beautiful to me because you always fight back. You're the strongest woman I know."

"I sure do fight back," Edna laughed, "don't I."

"I meant it in a good way." Russell kissed her. He looked her in the eyes and kissed her again. This time Edna kissed him back. They sat in the car, at the side of the road, on their way to Montana, and held each other. Finally, Russell turned the key in the ignition and started the car. They continued on their journey.

28

August 20, 1968

EDNA STAYED IN bed the morning after they arrived home from their wonderful trip. It was so depressing to be home. She didn't know why. She felt so blue, so despondent. She stared at the ceiling for a long time – thinking. If only she could turn her brain off... or just go back to sleep. Sleep was the perfect escape. She thought about taking a sleeping pill and just sleep the day away.

She glanced through the window. It was a nice day outside; David was up and had made himself breakfast. He had even made her a fried egg and a slice of toast and had brought it in quietly and set it down on the night table with a glass of orange juice. He was a dear, dear boy. But she felt so gloomy. She knew she should try to snap out of it.

She reached for the breakfast plate David had brought in and took a bite of the toast. She really didn't feel like eating. But she sat up and placed the plate on her lap and kept at it – one bite at a time. By the time she had finished and gulped down the glass of orange juice, she felt better. A little. She looked out the window at the bright blue sky and the puffy white clouds. Beautiful. It reminded her of Montana and her wonderful two weeks with her sweetheart. She closed her eyes and took her mind back… back to the river.

"Okay Edna – stand still. Don't move," Russell said, standing about 20 yards away from her. They both stood knee deep in the crystal clear, rushing water of the river and Edna had been instructed to stand with her right arm stretched straight out from her shoulder, holding Russell's hat out in the air. She looked at him and smiled. She absolutely was thrilled by his skill with a rod, some line, and a fly.

"I don't think you can do it," she teased.

"Oh you don't huh? Well, let's see… if I miss, I'll do the cooking tonight!"

Suddenly Russell's wrist flicked the grip of his rod and the line flew. Edna squealed as the fly caught the hat and it jerked right out of her hand. She jumped up and down, splashing water onto her blouse. "Hurray! I knew you could do it!"

Russell came trudging through the water towards her and pretended to be indignant as he said, "What! You just said you *didn't* think I could do it, you silly woman!" He grabbed her around the waist with his free arm and pulled her to him.

Edna rewarded him with a kiss and a repentant look on her face. "You could do that with your eyes closed."

"That's a good idea! Let's try it!" He handed her his hat, and began trudging through the water, back to his spot 20 yards away.

Edna stood still, incredulous, but willingly took his hat.

"I'm only kidding," Russell said with a huge grin. "You really would have stood there and let me try, wouldn't you have?"

Edna let out a relieved breath of air. "I thought you were serious!"

"Now that's trust." Russell had come back to her and once again pulled her to him and kissed her. "What do you say we go back to camp, clean ourselves up, and I'll take you to a restaurant for dinner tonight?"

"Sounds marvelous!"

Edna's thoughts returned to the present and she looked down at the empty plate on her lap. *The day is going to come and go no matter what I do*, she thought. *So, I might as well get up and do* something.

She walked into the kitchen and put the dishes in the sink. "David!" she called. "David!" she called again as she walked through the dining room to look for him. As she passed the dining table, her eye was caught by a vase of flowers and a note leaning up against it. She giggled as she noticed the lack of water in the vase.

> Dear H.G.,
>
> *I went for a walk this morning and found these lovely flowers that reminded me of you. I hope they brighten your day as you brighten mine. Thank you for a most wonderful time in Montana.*
>
> I love you dearly,
>
> S.D.

Edna kissed the note and leaned it back up against the vase. David had come in with the vacuum cleaner and was now vacuuming the dining room carpet. He seemed not to even notice Edna standing there. He paused for a moment at one of the chairs and said, "Sally lift up your feet." He vacuumed under Sally's feet then turned the vacuum off and said to the empty chair, "What's the matther Sally? You look pale." He paused, looking at the chair, then said so sweetly, "I *do* love you Sally." He paused again, then said, "Oh, good. Thank you Sally," and continued vacuuming. When he had finished, he went back to the dining room and flexed his arm muscles in front of the chair. "Feel it Sally. Feel it!" A few days earlier, Edna had watched David ask Sally to scratch his back. He looked as though he could feel his back being scratched. Then he had said, "Oh, that feelsth good Sally, that feelsth good." He turned around and said, "Thank you, Sally. Thank you."

"Davie dear, would you like to go to the library with me today and then I'll take you to lunch at McDonald's?" she asked him when he had turned off the vacuum.

He stared at her for a few moments without any expression, then finally said, "Yeth."

*   *   *

Edna and David stood in line at McDonald's behind a rather large black man who was dressed in a tan police officer's uniform and was carrying in his holster the biggest pistol Edna had ever seen. She felt small in comparison to him. She glanced over at David who looked puny in comparison. Edna felt nervous for some reason.

Suddenly, Edna saw a car drive up and park haphazardly at the entrance doors and two plain-clothes police officers jump out, leaving their doors wide open. They rushed through the doors and drew their pistols. Pointing their guns at the man in front of her they ordered him to come with them. One of them grabbed the man firmly by the arm and propelled him towards the doors. Without any resistance, the black officer calmly walked out with the other two men. They put him into the back seat of their car and sped away.

Edna was flabbergasted! She looked around her. No one else seemed to have paid any attention to the whole affair. She walked up to the counter, waiting for someone to say something about the astonishing event which had just taken place.

"May I help you?" the young man behind the counter smiled at her and asked. He was so pleasant.

"Did you just see that?" Edna asked him, befuddled with his apparent lack of concern.

"See what? Ma'am."

Edna looked around her again. David stood next to her, rocking back and forth, clacking his teeth and running his fingers through his hair. He kept muttering, "Hambuhguh. Hambuhguh."

Edna took a deep breath. "I guess I'll have two hamburgers and two French fries and two root-beers," she ordered. She looked around the restaurant again. Everything seemed to go on as if nothing had happened. People talked and the employees worked. What in the world was going on?

She and David sat down and ate their lunch. Normally, she wouldn't have stayed to eat; she was always conscientious of David's horrible eating habits – he made so much noise and ate with his mouth open all the time. She and Russell had corrected him his whole life, "Eat with your mouth closed," and "Don't burp at the table," "Don't let food drop out of your mouth," and "Please, take smaller bites." They had finally come to the conclusion that it was no use and usually left him alone about it. But eating in public was difficult – Edna felt as though people were staring at them and were disgusted by David. But this time, she didn't care. She wanted to stay and see if anything unusual happened. Nothing did. She was bewildered.

So, when they finished eating, they simply went home. Edna didn't tell Russell.

29

December 1969

BOB WAS IN Vietnam serving in the war and Ginny lived in a small home with the three children, a baby girl having been born just before Bob left. Ginny had wanted to be near Edna and Russell and David, but Edna wasn't doing well.

Ginny sat on the couch in the living room and looked down at Wendy, only 7 months old, who was sitting with a teether in her chubby hands and Ginny wished that Bob wasn't missing out on time with their newest addition. She reached down and stroked Wendy's adorable curly hair and looked over at Steven and Jill who were happily playing together in front of the television, when there was a knock on the door.

Ginny froze. She felt a knot in her stomach. *I hope that's not mother*, she thought. She tip-toed to the front door and drew back the curtain just enough to peek into the driveway where she saw Edna's blue Oldsmobile parked. Ginny quickly picked up baby Wendy from the floor and motioned to Steven and Jill to come with her.

Edna pounded on the door and shouted, "I know you're in there Ginny!"

Ginny led the three small children to the back of the house and closed the door to her bedroom behind them.

"What are we doing Mommy?" Steven asked, thinking they were playing a fun game.

"Well, we're going to play in my room for a little while."

"But I heard someone knock on our door." Steven ran to the bedroom door and shouted excitedly, "I'll go see who it is!"

"NO!" Ginny tried to shout without actually shouting loudly. "Steven, it was nobody we know, so we'll just stay in here until they go away."

"Was it a bad man? OR a monster?" Jill asked with big eyes.

"No, of course not. Let's play Simon Says!" Ginny tried to get their minds off "the person" at the front door.

For the last several months, Edna had become increasingly paranoid and delusional. She loved having Ginny so close again and had been visiting her several times a week to see the grandchildren. But Edna began acting so strange, so unpredictable, her behavior frightened Ginny. The last time Edna had come over, she was holding baby Wendy when she suddenly threw her to the floor and began screaming at Steven and Jill to, "Get away from it! Run! Run!" Steven and Jill started crying and screaming, backing themselves into the corner of the room. Wendy crawled off, bawling, and Edna ran into the kitchen, frantically opening every drawer.

"Mother, what in heaven's name is the matter? What are you looking for?"

Breathing heavily, Edna said, "A knife. I need a knife," as she continued opening all the kitchen drawers.

Ginny grabbed a glass full of cold water and quickly splashed her mother's face with it. Edna was so shocked that she abandoned her search for the knife. Ginny led her towards the front door, handing her a kitchen towel to dry her face. "Mother, Daddy just called and wants you to come home immediately," Ginny lied. It was all she could think of. She had to get her mother out of the house.

That evening Ginny called her father, "I just don't know what to do, Dad. I am afraid she'll hurt one of the children."

"You can't let her in anymore. Lock the doors, keep your curtains closed, and if she comes over again, don't answer the door. Even if she gets furious about it, don't let her in." Russell paused, then added, "Just remember, that's *not* your mother."

*   *   *

Edna got worse and worse. Russell prayed for help from heaven. A few months later, in February, Edna was in the back yard with David, when she became convinced that the neighbor was watching her from his window. She ran to the fence, climbed over it, and ran right into the neighbor's house, shouting that she wasn't going to stand for it anymore. She found her neighbor resting on his couch and she attacked him, wrapping her hands around his neck and shaking him. He was significantly larger than she, and quickly pushed her off, shouting for her to calm down. She continued yelling and screaming and lunged at him, attacking him again. He ran outside, got in his car and headed for Russell's store. Russell rushed home quickly and found Edna, still inside her neighbor's front room, on the floor crying. It was the final straw. Russell was able to coerce Edna into his car by telling her he was going to take her to Ginny's house, but instead drove to Rock Haven Sanitarium. He didn't feel he had any choice.

This time Edna was only there for two weeks; the help from heaven Russell had prayed for arrived. It was in the form of a new drug called Lithium. It had finally been approved by the FDA and Edna's doctor had prescribed it to her saying, "This new drug could change your life forever... if it works." Edna had been diagnosed some years earlier with *Manic-Depressive Disorder*. However, her doctor was not completely satisfied with the diagnosis, feeling that it didn't fully account for all of her symptoms, especially her delusions and paranoia. But she had been taking the new medication every day since she was admitted to Rock Haven and was amazed at the difference it was making.

After Edna had been home for a couple months, Russell was amazed too. She quit having her horrible, depressing days and he hadn't heard of any unusual sightings at the Market Basket, or of any wigged woman she was suspicious of, and she hadn't run into their neighbor's house to attack him again. Ginny let her come visit whenever she wished and the grandchildren all simply adored her. She seemed so... normal.

30

June 20, 1970

D AVID, ARE YOU ready to go?" Russell asked, peeking into his room from the hall. David turned around to face his dad and stared at him. He was buck naked, just standing there in the middle of his room. "David! What are you doing? You better get your swimsuit on and put your blue jeans on over it and a shirt. You can put your tennis shoes on in the car. We'll be late if you don't hurry." It was a silly thing to request of David, he had never *hurried* before in his whole life. He had one speed – SLOW.

"Russell darling, is David ready to go?" Edna called from the front door.

"He's dawdling, as usual," Russell hollered back.

Edna appeared at David's door. He was still just standing there in the buff. "Davie dear, don't you want to go to the pool for your big day? You've been practicing and practicing for this and your coach said you are really good!" David started rocking back and forth. "Don't you want to go swimming?"

David stopped rocking and looked up at Edna with big eyes. "Swimming?" he asked, as if he had been informed of the day's event for the very first time.

"Yes David. Swimming!"

"I love swimming!" David said with a big smile.

"Then get dressed and let's GO!" Russell said and handed David his speedo. David took it from him and put it on. He looked ridiculous in a speedo with his chubby belly spilling out over it, but his swim coach told him that's what he was to wear today rather than his usual swim trunks. The speedo was red, white, and blue, and when his coach had given it to David a week ago David had enthusiastically said it was, "Neato." From then on Edna and Russell had referred to it as his "neato speedo."

Finally arriving at the Belmont Plaza Olympic Pool in Long Beach, they dropped off David in the men's locker room with his coach. Edna looked at David and said, "Good luck Davie dear!" and leaned over to plant a kiss on David's forehead.

"I have a mouth," David said. So, Edna bent over and gave David a quick little peck on the mouth.

"Is that better darling?"

"Yeth," David said smiling.

Edna and Russell left the locker room and went to find their seats. Deanna and Cherie with their husbands, and Bobby Durfee, David's best friend, were all there to cheer him on. Many other families from David's school, which was now called *Villa Esperanza*, were there too. Some parents had children participating, but others had come just to watch and cheer on the kids from the school.

"Welcome to the Western States Regional Finals for the Special Olympics!" It was the voice of Mrs. Robert Kennedy over the loudspeaker and the crowd went wild with whoops and cheers. The cheering lasted for almost three minutes, then she was finally able to continue, "Two years ago, we had 1,000 participants. This year we have 50,000 participants, and two years from now we hope to have one million!" She paused to let the crowd cheer and holler again. "Let the games begin!"

It seemed like forever before it was David's event, but the big moment finally arrived. Russell squeezed Edna's arm as he spotted David coming toward the starting blocks wearing his neato speedo. "There he is!" Russell shouted excitedly. The Peak family clan and friends all cheered. David walked right past all the blocks and toward the exit door. But his coach caught up to him, turned him around and pointed to the third from the left starting block. David, looking at his coach, pointed at the block. The coach nodded his head and with his hand on David's shoulder, gently guided him up onto the block marked "3." David stood on the block and looked around. Edna wondered what he was thinking and if he was nervous. He didn't appear nervous at all and he wasn't rocking or clacking his teeth or running his hand through his hair. *He must be just fine,* Edna thought. She was the one feeling nervous for him. A few of the other swimmers took a very professional-swimmer-type pose and bent down to wait for the sound of the starting gun. David just stood on his block looking around.

BANG! Edna jumped in her seat as the gun went off. David dove into the water and everyone cheered. David swam his freestyle stroke remarkably well. He got quite a distance from the rest of the swimmers when he suddenly stopped and turned to the other boys and motioned for them to come. His coach told Russell and Edna later that day that he heard David say, "Come on felluhs!" David waited for a moment to let everyone catch up then kept swimming. He reached the end of the pool and stopped, turned around, and motioned again for the other swimmers to hurry. When the other swimmers reached the end of the pool David cheered for them.

At the end of the day, David stood at the top of the winner's podium with his gold medal hanging around his neck. He looked out blankly at the crowd but when he heard his name over the loudspeaker and the crowd cheering for him, he broke out into a huge smile and raised his hands up over his head.

David was a champion!

*　　*　　*

Two weeks later, Edna found David on his back on the living room floor, writhing and moaning in pain. "What hurts, David?" Edna desperately asked, trying to figure out what was wrong.

"My thumoch," David managed to finally say after a few long moments.

Russell came home immediately, and he and Edna took him to see their family doctor. The pains were diagnosed as stomach ulcers and a prescription for *Donnatal* was given to him.

Unfortunately, his condition precluded his going to Chicago for the International Special Olympics scheduled for August 13-15, at Soldiers Field. Of course Edna and Russell were the only ones who were disappointed – David didn't even know he was missing out on anything. But every night for what seemed like months on end, David would come into the living room in his neato speedo, with his gold medal hanging around his neck, and stand right in front of the TV that Edna and Russell were watching. David would acknowledge everyone in the room, "Muthuh, Dad, Sally," he would say as he nodded his head at Edna, Russell, and the empty chair next to them, "I got gold medal. I champion!"

"Yes, Davie dear. You are a champion."

31

July 1978

THE YEARS PASSED. David was now almost 30 years old, and Edna and Russell were in their 60's. But some things never change and one of those things was their love of Montana and their favorite places to camp and fish. This particular summer they took their annual camping trip and coupled it with an invitation Russell had received from Federal Judge Howard Smith, to come to his home in Missoula Montana and speak to a group of fishing enthusiasts.

"Welcome Mr. and Mrs. Peak. Thank you so very much for coming." Judge Smith greeted them as he shook their hands and led them into his large foyer. "And this must be your son, David." Judge Smith smiled wide at David, who smiled back and extended his hand to shake with the judge's.

"I Davith," he said as the judge took his hand and shook it warmly.

"Hi David. I'm glad you came with your folks."

Russell interjected, "We're a package deal."

Turning back to David, Judge Smith asked him, "Are you a fisherman like your dad?"

"I a polithman!" David answered.

"Why, that's a splendid thing to be!" Judge Smith winked at Edna and Russell and smiled kindly at David.

"He's always wanted to be a policeman ever since I can remember," Edna added.

A few more men came into the entrance hall, shaking Russ's hand, introducing themselves and expressing gratitude for the effort the Peak's had made to come speak to them.

As Russell was surrounded by the group of men, a female voice pierced through the chatter, "So, YOU'RE RUSS PEAK!" The men parted away from Russell enough to let the Judge's wife through. Judge Smith took her arm and motioned toward Russell to introduce her formally to him, but before he had a chance to speak, she suddenly fell on her knees and bowed down to Russell saying, "The way my husband talks about you, if you're not God, you're the next thing to him!"

The room filled with laughter and Russell's face turned red with humble embarrassment. He didn't exactly know what to do, so he took her elbow, raised her up, and said, "I assure you, I'm just a regular ol' person. And not a very exciting one at that." Russell introduced her to Edna and David. She was gracious, charming and funny, and Edna immediately liked her.

The group gathered in a large, beautifully furnished living room and Russell began speaking to them. David seemed bored until Mrs. Smith brought out several serving trays of sweets, cheeses, crackers, and vegetables. David spent the rest of his evening standing at the table, taking a brownie, then a cookie, then another brownie, then a cupcake. Edna kept her eye on him and finally went over to him, "Davie dear, you're going to get sick eating all these sweets."

"Sally wahnth's them," he said without looking at her. "Go sit down, Muhthuh," he ordered Edna.

Edna sighed, knowing there wasn't really much she could do to stop David from eating whatever he wanted, and when Sally was there, she knew she wouldn't be able to change David's mind about anything. But she felt she had to do her motherly duty and at least try. "Please eat a few of the vegetables David."

"Sally, you wahnth vegadubles?" he asked the air next to him. Edna rolled her eyes as David paused, looking at the air and waiting for an answer from Sally. "Sally saidth, 'no thank you' Muthuh." He turned his back to Edna and ignored her. Edna scratched her head and sighed again, deciding to let it go, and went back to her seat. From her seat she saw David pick up another cookie in his hand and heard him say, "Lose weight," as he put the cookie back on the platter. She was surprised that was even a thought in his head, but then let out an audible giggle when she heard him say, "Gain weight," as he picked the cookie back up and popped it into his mouth.

Russell talked about different flies: which ones to use for which fish, how to choose the best ones from stores, how to tie them properly, etc. etc… If she didn't love and admire him so much, she would have found herself grazing the table of sweets with David. But she liked to watch Russell talk – even if the topic *was* boring.

At the end of the evening, several of the men, including Judge Smith, asked Russell if they could join him the next day for a fishing demonstration at the river. Russell was thrilled to have the male companionship but turned to Edna and asked if she wouldn't mind.

"Of course I don't mind darling. I intend to work on a painting anyway.

*   *   *

Edna sat near the riverbank, with her canvas propped up on a rock and her paint supplies on a plaid blanket spread out next to her. The river was rushing from melted snow runoff and the banks were made up of mostly small pebbles. There were mountains far off in the distance, barely visible, and pine trees dotting the fields which surrounded the winding river. The sky was void of clouds completely and an occasional large black crow would fly overhead. Edna took in a deep breath of the fresh Montana air and closed her eyes to listen to the rushing water. Opening her eyes, she looked at the blank canvas propped against the rock, but she could see nearly every detail of what she felt inspired to paint. She had decided to attempt a watercolor this time and wanted to get it right.

David wandered around the riverbank, collecting leaves, rocks, and who knew what else, and stuffing each treasure into his pants' pockets. Edna told herself not to forget to empty his pockets when they got home, before washing his pants, something David never remembered to do on his own.

She gazed over at Russell and his posse. They were all squatting down with Russell, behind a cluster of bushes on the riverbank. Edna knew what Russell was going to do and couldn't help but giggle as she watched them all – grown men who looked like a bunch of rag-tag ten-year-old's, playing hooky from school in exchange for a day fishin' down at the river.

Russell motioned for everyone to be quiet. Edna stifled her laughter and could hear in her head the theme song to the television show *Mission Impossible*. Then Russell carefully placed the tip of his fishing rod through the bush and gave the grip a quick downward flick. His line went sailing out through the bush and into the middle of the river! The men cheered and whistled. Edna laughed; this was superb entertainment! But she wanted to get her painting started, so she dipped her brush into the blue paint and swept it across the canvas.

*   *   *

A couple years later, Edna's painting hung on the wall in Russell's store. It depicted Russell, standing thigh-high in a river, peacefully fishing. She had thought the painting amateur at best, and her painting instructor reminded her that she had a tendency to use a lot of black paint, creating a somber feeling. But Russell loved it and took it to his shop where he spent his days.

One Saturday a customer came in and poked around the store, looking at this and that. After allowing him ample time to look around, Russell approached him and asked him if he could assist him in finding something.

"Actually, I would like to buy that painting," the man said, nodding his head toward Edna's watercolor. "Would you take say... $300.00 for it?"

Russell looked at the man, then at the painting. "My wife painted that. I could never sell it."

The man continued to look at the painting, then dug into his back pocket and produced his wallet. "I understand. Why don't you ask your wife about it and if you change your mind, call me," and he handed Russell a business card.

Russell took the card and stared at it for a moment, he knew Edna would be flattered that someone wanted to buy her painting, especially offering so much money for it. S he would tell him adamantly, "SELL IT!" But he handed the card back to the man and said, "The painting is not for sale."

32

April 20, 1985

EDNA AND RUSSELL had lived through the springtime of their lives, with youth and the beautiful buds of courtship and love. The summer of their lives was adventurous and filled with excitement and challenges raising their four wonderful children. But just assuredly as the leaves will turn gold and fall from the trees, they too, had reached autumn.

It was their golden wedding anniversary, and everyone had come to the little house on Berkeley Avenue to celebrate it with them. Their 15 grandchildren were scattered about the house and backyard, coming in and out of the house as they pleased and filling the home and yard with chatter and laughter. David, however, was in his room with his door shut, sitting on the edge of his bed, rocking, clacking his teeth, and running his hand through his hair, his classic display of nervous tension.

Edna overheard one of the grandchildren, Shannon, open his door and try to coax him to come out. "David, don't you want to come and play with us?" Edna heard Shannon's little high-pitched voice say.

Then she felt badly when she heard David adamantly say, "NO! GO HOME!"

Edna rushed to his room and scolded, "David, Shannon was just trying to have fun with you. You need to be kind. Apologize to her."

David stared back and forth between Shannon and Edna, who were both standing in his doorway, staring at him and waiting. He kept rocking. He kept clacking. Finally, he stomped his foot on the floor and rolled his eyes, but reluctantly looked at Shannon and very insincerely said, "I sorry Shannon."

Shannon, who was seven years old, looked up at Edna and asked, "What's wrong with Uncle David? Why does he act different than everyone else?"

"Well dear, he has something called Down Syndrome."

Bouncin' Drums! What's Bouncin' Drums?"

Edna laughed. It was the cutest mistake. She rather liked *Bouncin' Drums*! "It's just something he was born with. He's special and he does things different than other people, but he can't help it. There are a lot of people with 'Bouncin' Drums'."

Shannon's sister, Kristie, had now appeared and asked, "What's Bouncin' Drums?"

Shannon looked at her and matter-of-factly said, "It's what Uncle David has, and he can't help it."

Kristie looked over at David, still sitting on his bed rocking, clacking, and stomping his foot, and said, "Oh!" and the two girls skipped down the hall and trotted off to join the rest of the children outside.

Edna sat down on the edge of the bed next to David. "Davie dear, I know it's hard for you to have the house so full of people, but you mustn't be rude to anyone. Alright?"

David stopped rocking and looked long and hard at Edna, giving her instructions some deep thought and finally reluctantly replying, "Okay okay, okay."

"Now, everyone wants you to come out of your room. Can't you do that? For Daddy and me?"

"Babiesth," David said.

"Daddy and I are babies?" Edna asked, confused.

"Noooo." David said and gave his mother his 'are you stupid or something' look. "I no like babiesth."

"Is that what you're worried about? No one has any little babies any more David, there won't be any crying. I promise." Edna was surprised this was his concern. There hadn't been a crying baby in the house for years now. David hated crying babies, it made him nervous and upset. Once, when Ginny brought the children over to the house, the baby at the time began to cry and David went up to it and demanded of it to "Shut up!" which made the crying only get worse, so he said again, "Shut up baby, shut up!" The crying turned into screaming and David clamped his hands over his ears and paced back and forth until Ginny finally came from the kitchen, scooped up the baby and soothed it, quieting the baby quickly.

"David, when the baby cries, you can just pick her up," Ginny had said.

"Go home Ginny," David had replied.

Edna stood up and patted David's head. "You just come out when you're ready. We all want you to come have cake and ice cream with us."

That did the trick. She had said the magic word. David's eyes practically popped out of his head. "Cake?!" David loved cake. No... David *adored* cake.

"Yes, David. Ginny and Deanna and Cherie all made a big three-layer cake for Daddy and me. It's beautiful. You need to come out and see it. The biggest layer at the bottom is your favorite: chocolate!" She said the word "chocolate" as if she were in a hit Broadway musical and "chocolate" was the grand finale jazz number.

David leapt off the edge of his bed and marched out of his

room in search of the giant cake. Edna went outside to announce it was time to come in and have cake and ice cream. Everyone began to pour into the dining room from the backyard and other parts of the house. And there in the center of the table was the beautiful anniversary cake the three daughters had made for their beloved parents, with an enormous slice missing from the bottom layer.

✳   ✳   ✳

Months earlier, when Edna and Russell discussed plans for their anniversary, they had insisted on a simple gathering in the backyard with hamburgers from *In-N-Out*. But Ginny, Deanna, and Cherie protested, saying, "That is no way to celebrate a golden anniversary." So, arrangements had been made and the family was gathered for a lovely dinner at a nice restaurant downtown. The tables were spread with white tablecloths and Deanna had brought a gorgeous flower arrangement of 50 yellow roses and had placed it in the middle of the long table.

Russell gazed down both sides of the table at his three daughters, sons-in-law, and his own son, and felt such joy, such contentment. He looked across the table at his sweetheart and was amazed that they were celebrating 50 years together. It felt like five. Edna had on a blue dress, the same color as the dress she had worn the day they got married. David had told her she looked "classy" when he saw her dressed to leave for the dinner. Russell thought she looked lovely in blue, especially now that her hair had turned white. Russell's hair was nearly gone, and they both had put on weight, proof of their love for See's Candy and the Eskimo Pies they always had in their freezer. They had both aged; their faces showed the time that had passed since their wedding day - their skin had thinned, and they had wrinkles and age spots just the same as every other older person. But Edna's eyes still twinkled when she smiled, and Russell's eyes were still the same piercing blue.

After diner, as the group chattered happily, Ginny stood and clinked her glass with her butter knife to gain everyone's attention. She held a small gold frame in her hands and once it had quieted down, turned to her parents and said, "Mother and Dad, I thought it would be perfect to read this tonight to everyone. It is the poem that Lars Mortensen, who married you, wrote for your marriage." Ginny looked at them both and then read the poem, now beautifully framed as an anniversary gift.

Why do two souls so oft meet
From climes so far apart?
And when they meet in bliss so sweet
Love springeth from their hearts.

Perhaps 'tis 'cause the Master, who
Our destiny he doth shape,
Would bring to meet two hearts so true
Because of love to mate.

To love, to live, and strive to gain
A mansion in Heav'n prepared,
Who'll find their efforts are not vain
For those who do and dared.

Their burdens will not be a load,
'Twill lead them back to God,
To live and love in joy supreme,
To be with the redeemed.

Everyone was deeply touched by the poem and Edna smiled at Ginny and said, 'Thank you darling. What a perfectly lovely gift. I remember that wonderful day 50 years ago. We went to Mr.

Mortensen's house where he was going to marry us. But he asked us to come in his car with him for a little ride. We didn't know what he was up to, but we went with him. He took us to the church building and when we walked in he had gathered a few friends there for us and had arranged for an organist to play Mendelssohn's *Wedding March*. He said he wanted us to have a proper church wedding. It was lovely. He read us a beautiful wedding ceremony and we were man and wife. He had even arranged for a soloist to sing our favorite song: *O Promise Me*. I don't even know how he knew that." Edna closed her eyes for a moment, remembering the tune, and humming softly. "I remember him giving us that lovely poem. What a dear, dear man he was."

Russell leaned over and tenderly kissed Edna on the cheek. "I remember the first time I saw my sweetheart. She was the prettiest girl I had ever seen and fifty years later, she's *still* the prettiest girl I know." Russell winked at Edna, who took hold of his hand and squeezed it. "Not very many people stay married for 50 years anymore," he continued, "it's a shame. They don't know what they're missing out on. 50 years is not enough for me. I want to be with my Honey Girl forever." With this, Russell abruptly ended, clearing his throat.

Edna gently patted his hand and said, "My Sweetheart Darling has loved me and loved me completely – even with all my faults. He has always treated me with such patience and kindness and gentleness, it boggles the mind." Edna paused for a moment and gazed at Russell. "These have been the best and happiest years of my life. I wish everyone could find a way to be as happy as we have been."

33

April 21, 1985

T
HE NEXT MORNING, Edna took her journal into the dining
room and set it down on the table next to her typewriter.
She had spent a little time typing her thoughts the evening
before their anniversary, while Russell was still busy at the store. He
was six years behind on his special orders and knew he wouldn't go
in on their anniversary day, so he had worked until 1:30 am. He was
currently trying to finish a rod for another Hollywood actor.

Russell had been declared as the *Stradivarius of Glass* as well as
the *Master of Glass* by authors of books and magazines. His rods
were claimed to be "*museum quality pieces, yet too wonderful as casting
instruments to gather dust in a collection.*" Everyone and anyone who
owned a Russ Peak rod actually fished with it. Edna was very proud
of him and his talent and accomplishments. He had worked hard
to become the expert that he was. She tried not to complain about
his late hours; he was a perfectionist and she loved him, *all* of him.

But Edna had pondered on the pet-peeves – things married
couples all have, and had written in her journal:

WHY I LOVE MY HUSBAND... REGARDLESS
OF THE FACT THAT:

1. He states the obvious... twice.
2. He putters.
3. If several small objects are on a table top or sideboard, he moves all of them, one by one, six inches to the left.
4. He talks:
   a. Shop.
   b. Religion if the subject comes up.
   c. Politics " "   "   " "
   d. News   " "   "   " "
   e. On the plus plus side, hilarious stories of his past experiences. (Does not belong on this list.)
5. He putters. (see #2.)
6. He makes LISTS.
   a. Loses the list.
   b. Forgets to look at the list.
   c. Procrastinates jobs on the list.
   d. Lectures me about making lists.
7. Pampers me like a fussy mother hen... but is that bad?
8. He is a terrible driver
   a. Weaves.
   b. Rushes up to stop signs.
   c. Crawls up to green lights.
   d. Drives too slowly... almost got a ticket for that.
   e. He has never had an accident. (Does not belong on this list.)
9. Interrupts to tell me the obvious. (See #1.)
10. Putters. (See #2 and #5.)
11. He is a workaholic (Horrid word!)
    a. Works night and day.
    b. Works just as long on his hobbies:

Making model airplanes.

Tying flies.

Making beautiful inlay work.

12. Reads:

    a. <u>Never</u> reads a novel.

    b. Readers Digest.

    c. Popular Mechanics.

    d. Religious scriptures and lessons. (a, b, and c make him fall asleep almost immediately.)

13. Seldom discusses anything unless I bring it up.

14. Telephones:

    a. Long, perhaps forty-five minute conversations with our children long-distance… I get about a two-minute report.

    b. His customers call me by mistake. (This does not always bother me, however. Only if I am in the middle of doing something.)

15. He is kind, thoughtful, loving, generous, and unselfish… which makes me feel like a witch!

After rereading the list she had written she sighed. It was all true, but she knew it was only half of the truth. Edna got up from her chair and went to the kitchen for a cup of hot chocolate she had simmering on the stove. When she came back into the dining room, David had taken the cushion she used to ease her back pain and replaced it where it belonged on her sitting chair. "David, I still need that cushion." He fetched the cushion and, placing it back on the chair at her typewriter said, "Getting old." *He is correct about that,* she thought, sitting down and inserting a new sheet of paper into the typewriter. Edna's fingers began to fly again across the typewriter keys:

A Sequel To The Above List
MY HUSBAND LOVES ME REGARDLESS
OF THE FACT THAT:

1. I talk too much.
   a. I wait for a commercial on TV but talk on into the program.
   b. I begin an animated conversation in the car just at the point Russell should be turning off the freeway, causing him to miss it.
   c. I make long, long-distance calls to our daughters.
2. I like to argue. (This is probably a continuation of the above.)
   a. I guess I pout when I am bested.
3. I am stubborn.
4. I eat too much candy and white bread.
5. I am not a meticulous housekeeper.
6. Quite the opposite from my dear husband, I am a loner.
   a. I am most happy reading, writing, watching TV, going for short rides – or long rides – if I can avoid people.
7. According to S.D. I read the wrong things.
   a. Non-fiction: James Herriot, Andy Rooney, Jack Smith, etc.
   b. Fiction: Margaret Truman, Agatha Christie, Mary Stewart, etc.
   c. Newspapers, magazines, especially crossword puzzles.
   d. My husband hints pointedly that I should read scripture and the Sunday-school Manual regularly. But I don't.
8. I pamper the cat.
9. If opposites attract, this may be why my husband loves me. He is very patient, I am not.
10. I have written about envy, that "green-eyed monster" in my journal. Related is another monster, jealousy. I felt that emotion strongly at one time and it was entirely unwarranted. It is a most miserable state and one to be avoided if possible.

Edna finished her list and was looking it over, feeling it was unfair that Russell's list was longer, in spite of the fact that she was the one with more faults. But she couldn't concentrate anymore because across the table from her, David was having an argument with Sally and she couldn't help but want to hear what it was all about.

"Don'th hit me!" David held the side of his face. "Oh yeth you did!" he raised his voice at the empty chair next to him with consternation. "Ith over, over, over!" He pretended to ignore the empty chair. Then he took his wallet from his pocket and said, "Oh, you wanth more?" and held out two *Monopoly Game* $100 dollar bills. He held them out for a few minutes, waiting. "Never mindth," he said as he put the money back into his wallet. "Now I crying," he said as he began to fake-cry.

Edna laughed at his antics, causing him to look up from his lover's quarrel.

"Muthuh, Sally mad ath me."

"Maybe you should give her a kiss and tell her you're sorry." Edna went along with David's imaginary fight. Apparently, David watched too much TV - she and Russell had never argued over money.

David leaned over to the next chair and puckered up. He froze in the goofy position, but finally turned back to Edna and said, "She wonth kisth me."

"You didn't tell her you're sorry."

He turned back to the chair and said, a little half-heartedly, "I sorry, Sally." Suddenly he jerked his head back as he exaggeratingly received a kiss, and then his broad smile spread out across his face. "She kisth me, Muthuh!" He smiled at the chair and repeated, "I sorry, Sally." He jerked his head back again and smiled his huge smile. "I sorry, Sally." David was anxious to apologize now and very enthusiastic about the results.

Edna left the apologizing and kissing David at the table and walked into the kitchen for a glass of lemonade. She could still hear David in the dining room: "I sorry, Sally."

Returning to her journal, she added a final entry for the day:

It is a wonder that we have been married over fifty years. Russell still brings me flower bouquets accompanied by love notes, he takes me for short rides often in order to get me out of the house. He does the strenuous housework, takes David to school, does all the marketing. He remembers all the special days (birthdays, Mother's Day, Valentine's Day, and Christmas.) He spends all his kisses.

34

January 30, 1989

D AVID WAS TURNING 40! Edna and Russell spent the
morning decorating the picnic table in the backyard for his
party and Edna had made him his favorite chocolate cake.
It had a figurine of a boy set on top and a bowling ball she had made
out of a red gumball, and pins made out of *Good and Plenty* candy.
She was quite proud of her confectionary display of David's favorite
thing to do, and she knew he would love it. She had even hidden it
from him down in the cellar where she knew he would never go. He
was scared of the cellar. He had only ventured down into it once in
his whole life when he was four years old and had refused to go back
for the past 36 years.

The front doorbell rang and Russell opened the door. Standing
on the other side of the screen was David's best friend, Bobby Durfee,
holding a box wrapped up in bright red paper with choo-choo trains
all over it. Bobby smiled his big smile and said cheerfully, "Hi Misuh
Peak!"

"Well, hello Bobby!" Russell opened the screen door and Bobby
came right on in; the Peak's was his second home. Passing Edna,

he said brightly, "Hi Linda!" Edna had mentioned years earlier to Bobby that she didn't like her name, and from then on, he had called her Linda. He put the present down on the dining room table and went straight through the hall to David's room where David sat on his floor, going through his record collection. The two listened to records together until the rest of David's friends had all arrived.

Outside, the group of buddies sat around the picnic table. As usual there was a gap in the seating arrangement right next to David. Everyone had gotten used to the fact that David would insist no one sit in "Sally's spot."

All of David's guests had on birthday cone hats with the elastic way too tight under their chubby chins and some were busy blowing the noisemakers, watching the paper roll out and roll back in with their breaths. All of David's friends were actually adults, most in their 30's, but they were all children, never aging, never growing old, never tiring of the simple joys in life. When David was born, the average life span of someone with Down syndrome was only 12 years old, and even decades after that it was only 25 years old; mostly because they were usually institutionalized and treated badly. For David to reach his 40th birthday was a happy occasion, and Edna and Russell were so grateful that he was still healthy as a horse.

In the middle of the happy chatter and laughter, Edna began singing, "Happy birthday to you," while Russell carried David's birthday cake to the table and placed it in the center, in front of David.

"For ME?" David exclaimed, once the singing had finished.

"Yes of course it's for you David. It's YOUR birthday!"

"Oh boy!" David said, looking at the colorful cake. "I bowling! I love bowling! Thank you Muthuh."

"Make a wish David."

David stared at the cake while the candles burned. He stared longer. The candles kept burning. Finally, he said loud and clear, "I with I wath TALL!" and he blew out the flames that were hanging on for dear life in their individual puddles of wax. Every year he made the same wish. Edna had given up on telling him not to say it out loud.

"Your wish won't come true if you say it out loud David." He would just look at her with a blank stare. Certainly, it didn't make any sense to him.

"Why?" he asked.

"Well, because… Oh for heaven's sake, what in the world does it matter. You go ahead and tell the whole world David," she had finally said one year. Everyone knew that he was going to wish he was tall anyway. Not saying it out loud was just some silly tradition that who-knows-who made up for who-knows-what reason.

Everyone was digging into their slices of chocolate cake with pure joy and David had Edna slice a piece for Sally and place it in front of her on the table. It was a cinch to please this group. One would have thought they had all died and gone to heaven to see them devouring that cake. They all had chocolate, white frosting, and candy bits all over their teeth, lips, nose, cheeks, and chins. They all wanted seconds; they all *got* seconds. David got thirds because, as he had told Edna, Sally didn't want hers. So he ate it for her.

"Thank you Muthuh," David said after the cake had been demolished.

Edna smiled happily as she heard an echo of "Thank yous" from around the picnic table.

"Would you like to open your presents now darling?"

"YETH!"

David carefully pulled off the tape and unwrapped the paper from around the box Bobby had brought. He refolded the paper and handed it to Edna, who placed it carefully in a box to be reused.

David shouted with joy, "Look Muthuh! Look Daddy!" He held up a plastic softball and a vinyl mitt.

"My, what a wonderful time you boys will have with that! What do you say to Bobby, Davie?"

David turned himself to face Bobby and threw his arms around his neck, giving him a huge hug while saying, "Thank you Bobby!"

Ginny and Bob had sent David a birthday card and a check for $10. He handed the check to Russell, and Edna asked David what he wanted to get with the check, to which he replied, "I want the money."

David opened all his gifts: new white socks, two new records, a big bag of his favorite *Reese's Peanut Butter Cups*, and a yellow t-shirt that said, "I'm Happy, How 'bout You?" on the front. David was so happy he cried. David always cried opening gifts.

✳   ✳   ✳

That evening after everyone had gone home and the little house on Berkeley Avenue was quiet once again, Edna and Russell took a short stroll down the street together. Edna's arthritis was getting so painful it was a rare treat to feel well enough to go for a walk.

"Your cake was delightful, dear," Russell complimented her.

"Thank you darling. You know I don't usually go to such extravagant extremes, but I thought it would be fun this year for such a special birthday."

They walked slowly a little further, hand in hand.

"Did I tell you what happened to me the other day when I went for my hair cut?" Russell asked.

"No, you didn't. What happened?"

"Well, I had to go to the bank, and to the barber shop to get a haircut. I decided for some reason to put off going to the bank until after the haircut. I guess what little is left was tickling my neck." Russell stroked the remaining hair left on the back of his head. "After the haircut I went to the bank and was astonished to find out that a robbery had taken place just moments before I got there. Everyone was still in shock from it and the police were there questioning the tellers and customers. Boy was I glad I had gone to the barber shop first!"

"My heaven's Russell! Not any gladder than I am!" Edna squeezed Russell's hand. "What in the world would I do if something ever happened to you?"

The pair walked in silence for a few moments, enjoying the misty California evening and the orange glow of sunset. "We're getting old, aren't we Russell?"

"Speak for yourself my dear!" Russell teased.

"Some days I still feel 25," Edna looked at Russell the same flirty way she had when they were young and falling in love, "Other days I feel 100," she added with a sigh.

"I know what you mean. It's a strange thing, isn't it? My whole life it was *other* people who were old – not *me*. As a young man, I never gave one thought to things like going bald, getting fat," Russell patted his stomach, "or not being strong and agile. I guess I took youngness for granted. At least I'm not going senile." Russell chuckled as he added an afterthought, "YET, anyway!"

Russell suddenly gave Edna's hand a squeezing signal to stop for a moment and pointed to a little squirrel scampering up a tree. "The squirrels are sure out and about these days, aren't they?"

35

February 1, 1989

TWO DAYS LATER, Edna sat at the picnic table in the backyard reading the newspaper. David was in the house folding and putting away the laundry which was one of the chores he had been doing for his mother for years. She looked up from the paper for a minute and marveled at what a poor job she had done cleaning up the table after David's birthday party. There were crumbs everywhere and frosting smeared on the plastic tablecloth still covering the table. A few party hats and noisemakers lay on the ground, table and bench. She shrugged it off and decided to clean the mess up after she finished reading the paper.

The headline that day read: *Squirrel Goes Nuts, Terrorizes Neighborhood With Its Attacks.* Edna thought the title curious and decided to read the article, which described a tiny grey squirrel gone berserk. *This was no docile, park-variety peanut eater...* Edna smiled as she read on, *Beneath its soft, smoky fur flecked with bright orange, throbbed the mind of a rodent apparently gone mad.* Edna couldn't help but think that perhaps the squirrel just needed a little lithium. She continued to read about the squirrel's victims – all women minding their own business, when they were suddenly attacked by the ornery little critter. One woman was hanging laundry outside on the line when the squirrel jumped on her and began scratching and biting her. Another victim, a teenager, was bit while sitting on her front porch and when her mother came out to help, the pesky squirrel bit her too. Edna shook her head, thinking now that the squirrel might do well with some shock therapy! The article went on, describing one woman being attacked while putting out food for the cute little squirrel, unaware of its criminal past. Upon finishing the article, Edna was relieved to learn that the squirrel had been captured and *drugged with chloroform and wrestled into custody, but died a short time later without giving its side of the story.* Edna put down the paper and watched Russell, who was up on a ladder, trimming their rather out-of-control persimmon tree.

Within moments, out of the corner of her eye, Edna noticed a squirrel scamper across their driveway toward the yard. She looked right at him. He stared right back and then began to make an awful screeching, shrieking type of noise. Edna looked over at Russell who was oblivious to the angry squirrel. Edna squeezed her eyes shut. She couldn't possibly actually be seeing this. She opened her eyes only to find the ready-to-pounce squirrel still there. Certainly she was imagining this. She was well aware that, before taking lithium, she used to see things that weren't really there. Usually though, it was people.

Suddenly, the squirrel ran right up to the picnic table and jumped up onto it at the opposite end from Edna. Edna screamed in fright. Surely it was another woman-attacking squirrel. The squirrel shrieked and scampered off just as Edna looked over at Russell who had been so startled by her scream that he lost his balance on the ladder. Edna let out a much more frantic scream as she helplessly watched Russell tumble off the ladder and fall to the concrete driveway below. Horrified, Edna rushed over to him. "Oh dear

God, Russell! Russell!" she yelled out as she hurried to get to him. As she approached his limp figure lying in the driveway, she saw blood oozing from his head. She screamed for David who, thankfully, heard her and came to the back porch door. "David, go next door and get Mr. or Mrs. White. And HURRY!" David looked at Edna, then at Russell who was now moaning. "David, please, HURRY!" Edna lifted Russell's head onto her lap and caressed his cheek. "Oh Russell, I'm so sorry I frightened you!"

Russell moaned and managed to say a weak, "My head." It wasn't much, but Edna was grateful that he was conscious and talking.

Moments later Mr. White came hobbling down the driveway with his cane. "Edna, what happened?" he asked, looking at Russell's bleeding head.

"Russell fell from the ladder. I'm not sure what to do."

Mr. White pointed to his house with his cane and said, "My son is here visiting, he can help us get Russ in the car and we'll take him to the hospital." With that, Mr. White hobbled off, leaving Edna holding Russell's head in her lap and David nervously rocking as he looked down at his dad.

*   *   *

Edna sat in a chair at Russell's side, holding his hand. He was awake and complaining about having to stay at the hospital overnight.

"I really feel just fine dear," he said, trying to convince Edna.

"Russell darling, the doctor said they need to observe you over night to be sure you're alright. You had a dozen stitches put in your head and they said there could be damage that they can't see."

"The x-ray was fine." Russell had no patience for being a patient.

"Are you arguing with me?" Edna winked at him and patted his hand. "I know you want to go home, but you are simply going to have to put up with staying here. Just for one night."

Russell sighed knowing it was no use and he would simply have to accept his fate. "Where's David," he asked.

"He was quite upset about you, so Bobby's mother came and picked him up and will keep him at their house for the night. I'm sure he'll feel comforted being at the Durfee's."

"I can't believe I fell off a ladder. I spent 20 years on ladders when I was a painter," Russell said with disgust at his clumsiness.

"Well, you are not a young man anymore, now are you darling?"

"I guess this proves it, doesn't it?"

*   *   *

The fall proved to be something else as well – a blessing, in a strange kind of way. After thoroughly examining Russell's head once more before allowing him to go home, the doctor found several concerning growths, possibly cancerous. A biopsy revealed that they were indeed, and Russell underwent surgery three days after the fall. One of the growths had attached itself to his skull, so they removed a portion of the skull itself to be certain they had removed everything and anything cancerous. Once the ordeal was over, the bandages removed, and the stitches out, a sizable dent remained on the top left side of Russell's head. Russell just took it all in stride, joking that Edna had clocked him a good one.

36

August 1990

RUSSELL TOOK A long, deep breath. The air was so incredibly clean and fresh in Montana. Looking at his favorite fishing spot along the Madison River, he stood on the bank for a while, just watching the river water flow past him. He never tired of rivers – this one in particular. It was almost as if they were alive, with a soul and something to say to everyone who visited. He listened carefully to the sounds, the rushing water, birds chirping, the rustle of leaves and cracking branches.

Cutting through the sounds of nature, Ken called to him, "Come on Russ, get your old self in! We got some fishin' to do!" Ken had been a good friend for a long time, he and Russell had shared a lot of adventures together. One time, near this very spot, Ken had gotten out of the river before Russell and was resting back in their tent for a while. When he returned to the river, he saw Russell a short distance downstream, standing at the riverbank, staring straight into the face of a bull moose. Ken froze, not knowing what to do. He knew an animal that large could kill Russell in an instant if it had a mind to. Russell just stood, holding his rod by his side, staring the moose straight in the eyes. The moose finally simply dropped his head, turned, and sauntered away.

Ken was once again fishing with his old friend on, what Russell expected, was to be his last fishing trip. He was starting to have some problems… problems with his memory. Oh, it didn't seem to be much of a big deal, he just forgot things now and again. Little things, like the other day he had asked Edna where David was.

"I just told you a minute ago dear, he's at Bobby's house," Edna had patiently replied.

Russell tried to remember her telling him, but he couldn't. Oh well, he had thought, it's no big deal.

Now he stood at the edge of his favorite place in the world. He could never, ever, forget this river. His memory was a little weakened with age, but his body was still fairly husky and strong and Russell had no problem trudging through the water until he was thigh-high in the middle of the gently rushing water. This was home. This was heaven. He checked the fly and the line and began to survey the river for just the right spot to cast out his line. A bald eagle flew overhead and screeched. Russell looked up and marveled at the beauty of the sight. It was always a thrill to see the magnificent national bird and he saw at least one nearly every time he came to Montana. The sky was a brilliant blue, with a few white, puffy clouds scattered here and there. *Big Sky Country*, Russell thought, *it's so fitting. Somehow, the sky really is bigger here.* He looked around at the tall, mature ponderosa pine trees that dotted the banks of the river and breathed in another long, satisfying breath of fresh air, then gave the grip of his fishing rod a quick flick. At 78 years old he was just as graceful and skilled a fly fisherman as he had ever been.

Russell watched his line gracefully dance back and forth through the air, the fly skimming the water for only a second and then dancing again back through the air. He repeated the motion over and over, until instinctively, he let the fly settle in the water.

Within moments the line went taut and Russell jerked back on the line to secure the hook into the fish's mouth. The fishing rod arched until his handmade glass rod looked as if it would break in two. As he turned the handle on the reel to bring in his catch, he began to think about Edna, and David, and himself. They were so much like his fishing rods: remarkably fragile, and yet remarkably strong all at the same time. They could bend until it appeared they would break. But they didn't. They always managed to get through hard times - even things that sometimes bent them to their bitter extreme. But they never broke. They always managed to return back to their full strength, capable of accomplishing whatever they had to. No matter how difficult the challenge, they always won the prize in the end and not only survived the hardships of life, they found the joy in life: each other.

37

July 1994

I T'S AMAZING HOW one small accident that happens in just a few quick moments, can change not just one life, but many. So it was with Russell's fall from the ladder. Four years later, his ability to remember anything was about as long as it had taken him to fall.

After 53 years, the store at 21 N. Allen Avenue was sold and Russell retired. He had enough orders for 7 years of work, but Russell's memory had become an obvious problem and Ginny had traveled down to Pasadena to help with the necessary arrangements. She also wrote to every single customer he had in his files, informing them that Russell's store had been sold and thanking them for years of loyalty.

It was a difficult transition for Russell. Most days he still arose around 6 a.m., got dressed in his usual work clothes: plaid short-sleeve cotton shirt, khaki pants, and comfortable black shoes. Edna would rouse from her sleep, hearing him moving about, and would find him at the dining room table, eating a bowl of cereal and reading the paper. She would remind him that he had sold the store, retired, and didn't need to get up so early anymore. He would calmly laugh at himself – that he could forget something like that, and respond the same way every time, "Some habits are just hard to break," and then continue eating his cereal and reading the paper, ten or fifteen minutes later rising from the table and continuing his morning routine, Edna reminding him again and again that he was retired and Russell responding again with a chuckle and his reply, "Some habits are just hard to break."

One time, a new acquaintance had asked Russell what he had done for a living. Edna had been completely flabbergasted at his reply: "I was a painter all my life." It saddened her heart deeply to think that his memory of rod making was being erased. He was now 82 years old, Edna was 85, and David was a very youthful 45.

*   *   *

Ginny and Bob, who had retired from the Marine Corps and had moved to a tiny town in Montana called Bigfork, drove down to Pasadena to take the "three-legged stool," as they referred to Edna, Russell, and David, on a trip. Ginny stood at David's bedroom door, frustrated. "David, you have to get dressed. The motor home is all packed and Mother and Dad are almost ready. You're not even dressed." David stood in the middle of his bedroom with his favorite outfit on: white socks pulled up as hard and high as he could pull, with the sock heels coming up to about mid-calf, and whitey-tighty underwear, pulled up as hard and high as they would go. He just didn't look right.

"I not going," David said.

"Why not?"

David just stood and rocked back and forth, clacking his teeth as usual and running his hand through his hair – starting at his forehead and ending at the crown of his head.

"David, why don't you want to go? It will be fun! Bob and I are taking you and Mother and Dad on a big trip to Yellowstone. It will be the last time Mother and Dad get to see it. Don't you want to make them happy?"

David stared at Ginny and gave her his classic evil eye. He finally said in almost a whisper, "Sally." Then he echoed, "Sally… Sally… Sally…"

Ginny's eyes widened, "David, do you want Sally to come too? Is that what you're upset about?"

"Yeth." David stopped rocking. He stopped clacking and his hand fell to his side.

Ginny went to David and put her arm around him, "Sally can come! We have plenty of room for her."

David looked up at Ginny and grinned. "I get dresth now."

Relieved that the problem was solved, Ginny went in the dining room where Bob was telling Russell for the hundredth time where they were going.

"Ginny and I are taking you and Edna and David on a trip in our motor home to Yellowstone," Bob said, trying to hide the irritation in his voice.

"Oh boy! That sounds swell." Russell walked back into the kitchen and got himself an *Eskimo Pie* from the freezer. Coming back into the dining room, he looked at Bob and Ginny and asked, "What's going on? It looks like you two are going somewhere."

Bob looked at Ginny and rolled his eyes, "Oh my gosh," he said under his breath, "It's *your* turn. Maybe he'll remember if *you* tell him. AGAIN."

Ginny looked at Russell. "Dad, we're taking you on a trip. Remember?"

"Oh boy! Why I love going on trips! Where are we going?" he asked as he unwrapped the chocolate covered ice cream bar and took a huge bite.

The five of them, six including Sally, had not gotten out of the driveway when Russell asked where they were going. It was going to be a LONG three weeks.

*   *   *

Edna and Ginny sat together at a small table in the back of the motor home. They had enjoyed the last few hours together, talking and looking out the windows at the scenery. But the conversation had lost its light-heartedness. Edna softly cried and wiped the first tear that dropped as fast as it fell.

"I feel so darn guilty for getting so irritated and impatient with him. I love him so dearly and he has always been so patient and loving to *me* our whole lives even though I've been beastly to live with at times. But his incessant questions drive me crazy."

"I hope not literally Mother!" Ginny giggled.

Edna couldn't help herself from laughing too, even as she wiped more tears. "No, thank heavens *that* problem is under control."

"Seriously, Mother. Don't feel badly. Anyone that is around Dad at all knows how frustrating it is. Go ahead and get mad at him if you need to. He won't remember a thing! I think it's literally impossible for you to make him feel bad or hurt his feelings. If you did, he would forget that you had about 30 seconds later."

"More like 10." Edna and Ginny both laughed and then turned the conversation to the grandchildren and great-grandchildren.

Up front, Bob was driving and trying to show interest in Russell's story he was telling for about the twentieth time.

"When I was working as a painter I had the occasion to do some painting for the famous opera singer Maria Jaritza." Bob said the name in unison with Russell. "How did you know who I was going to say?" Russell looked at Bob in utter amazement.

"Just a lucky guess, Dad." Bob answered – again.

"Well, she was a nut. And she had a bad temper. One time she took some of my paint brushes – very fine red sable brushes I had managed to collect over a period of time. She just wanted them because they looked like fine brushes, she had no use for them," Russell said with disgust. "When I accused her of taking them, she refused to give them back, saying she had paid for them. So, I told her I would take feathers from her fine collection of birds. She got angry and hid my brushes in her wine cellar. So, I went right on out and plucked all the feathers off the tops of the heads of all her birds." Russell chuckled at his own story as he sat remembering the incident so long ago.

"They sure did look funny – all bald!" Bob finished the story in the same words Russell had finished it with every previous telling.

Russell glanced up at Bob, confused, utterly confused. Then his confused expression faded, and he looked down, shook his head, chuckled, and said, "They sure did look funny – all bald!" Russell looked up at Bob, laughing, expecting Bob to laugh.

There was a brief reprieve from the continuous talking before Russell leaned over in his seat, trying to get a glance at the gages on the dashboard. "How's your gas, Bob?"

"My gas is fine. How's yours?" Bob asked back.

Russell laughed as he realized the wording he had asked the question with and answered, "Swell!"

Russell was quiet for a moment, then he leaned over and, looking at the gages asked, "How's your gas, Bob?"

"Oh my gosh," Bob muttered under his breath. "Someone shoot me. Or him." Bob took a very deep breath and answered, "We have more than half a tank, Dad. A half-gallon less than the last time you asked," he answered loud enough to be sure Russell heard.

"Well that's good. Have I ever told you about the time I painted a house for the famous opera singer Maria Jaritza?"

"YES! Yes, you've told me that one. Why don't you tell me

about someone else. Can you remember doing a painting job for *anyone* else, Dad?" Bob was desperate not to hear the same story again. "What other painting jobs did you do?"

"Painting jobs? You want to hear about my painting jobs?"

Here it comes, thought Bob, *Maria Jaritza – again.* Bob sighed and braced himself.

"One time I did a job for an extremely wealthy man who owned a large estate in Pasadena."

Bob was shocked to hear a new story.

"When I arrived, the servant told me I would have to wait until the 'Master' had had his breakfast," Russell continued. "So, I wandered outside around the grounds, mad that I was being asked to wait. I found an old gentleman in dirty overalls, apparently the gardener, and asked him about the 'old bastard' who owned the place. You can imagine my shock when the old fellow said, 'I AM the old bastard who owns the place!" Russell laughed. Even Bob laughed. His stories *were* funny – the first time.

*   *   *

Three days later Bob, Ginny, Russell, and Edna were sitting along the riverbank, enjoying a picnic lunch Ginny had prepared, when they noticed David. He had climbed up to the top of a rock about four feet high and was standing there, facing them, like Lewis without Clark, discovering the new territory.

Ginny nudged Edna, "Look at David, Mother. What's he doing?"

David reached in the back pocket of his jeans and pulled out an imaginary… something. He fiddled around with it and then, with his index finger and middle finger held together in a "V" he lifted… oh, a cigarette to his lips and inserted it into his mouth. He returned the imaginary cigarette pack to his back pocket and squinted at the sun in his eyes, even though the sun was behind him. But it looked cool. Then he took a "match" and scraped it with lightning speed across his right hip and "lit" his cigarette. He puffed a few long ones. The audience roared. There he was, Mr. Suave, Mr. Cool. Standing on his four-foot rock, squinting into the sun.

At that moment, David *was* the Marlboro Man.

*   *   *

Later that afternoon, just after Bob had filled the tank of the motor home with gas and was waiting to turn out of the station parking lot, Russell leaned over to Bob and asked, "How's your gas Bob?"

38

September 1997

IT HAD BEEN three years since Bob and Ginny had taken Russell, Edna, and David on the trip to Yellowstone, returning them back home to Pasadena, and then making the two-day drive back to Montana themselves. But now, Ginny was back in her childhood home, watching Edna's strange behavior. She thought back to the three-week trip and wished that things could have just stayed the same. But they didn't.

"Mother, what in heaven's name are you doing?" Ginny asked as she watched Edna poke a fishing rod around and around into the opening of the attic.

"Deanna and Gary are in there and they're being held captive. I'm trying to help them."

Ginny's brow furrowed. "But Mother, there's no one up there."

Edna glared at Ginny and yelled, "OH YES THERE IS!" Edna turned her attention back to the opening and continued to poke the fishing rod around. "I have to save them. They're going to die."

"Mother, please. Come with me and I'll take you for a ride in the car," Ginny gently pleaded. "We can go to *In-n-Out* and get lunch. Please Mother, come with me." Ginny was desperate to try and calm her. She looked down at the laundry basket sitting in the hall next to Edna. That morning she had noticed it, packed with food and other items, and had asked Edna about it. "It's supplies for Deanna and Gary," she had replied. Ginny had shrugged it off, but now she understood.

"Where's Russell?" Edna began to hobble around the table toward the kitchen. Now 88 years old, she was getting thinner and thinner, her arthritis was terrible, but worst of all, she had quit taking her lithium a few months earlier. Their insurance had changed to an HMO and wouldn't allow her to see the psychiatrist she had been seeing for the past 30 years and her prescription needed to be refilled and required a doctor's approval – a doctor who was on the HMO list. She so desperately didn't want to rehash her entire life problems and history to a new doctor, that she had decided she could simply let her medication run out. She had been on it for so many years that certainly it wouldn't really matter. She was terribly wrong.

The real problem was that Edna thought she was fine. But she was no longer rational and had no idea how out-of-whack she had become. She was delusional, paranoid, angry and even violent. Just the other day she had thrown a glass at Russell's head again. She missed, thank goodness, or he may have ended up with another dent in his head. His memory was so nonexistent that he just kept asking, "What's the matter with you Honey Girl?" She would scream at him, "Don't call me that!" Two minutes later he would ask the same thing. That's how the glass got thrown.

Ginny was frightened enough by her mother's behavior that at night she would push the dresser up against the door, safeguarding herself against Edna coming into the room in the middle of the night while she slept.

A couple weeks earlier, a close and trusted friend of the family's from church had finally called Ginny and Bob. "I don't know how to help her. She just simply won't listen to me. Or anyone. I think you better come down and see if she'll listen to you," he had said.

Ginny had flown down as soon as she could make arrangements to see if she could get her mother to take her medication. She had begged, pleaded, and even bribed her. All unsuccessfully.

Today, she had decided to try hiding it in Edna's food. Ginny placed the plate of chicken and potatoes in front of Edna who was so paranoid that she wouldn't eat it, accusing her, "You're trying to poison me, aren't you? You want to get rid of me."

"Mother, I love you! I'm here to *help* you."

"You can't help me," Edna said humbly. Ginny thought that for just one moment perhaps her mother would listen to reason.

"Mother, you will feel so much better if you take your lithium again. Dad and David still depend on you. They need you."

"I'm FINE!" Edna was adamant and upset again. "I don't need any medication," she said as she rose from the table and hobbled around the family room, looking behind furniture and peeking out the closed drapes. "I have to protect all of us. There are people out there, spying on us." She went to the TV and turned it on and off, over and over. Then hobbled around it, checking the wiring. She looked back at Ginny and said, "They're in the TV too, you know."

"Who? What are you talking about Mother?"

"People are spying on us through the TV. I don't know how they do it though. I can't figure it out..." Edna began turning the TV on and off again.

Ginny shook her head and went to check on David. He spent most of his days in his room, avoiding his mother. When Ginny opened his door, she found him lying down on his bed, making out with the pretty girl on a record cover. He paused momentarily to look at Ginny, then returned to his flat girlfriend.

"David, dinner is ready. Come on out and have some, OK?"

She heard a muffled "OK" so she gently closed the door and went out to the backyard to find Russell.

"Dad, would you like some dinner?"

"Sounds swell. What are we having?"

"Chicken and potatoes," Ginny answered as she led Russell back into the house. As they went through the porch door Russell said, "I sure am hungry. Any chance we can have some dinner?"

"Yes Dad. We're having chicken and potatoes."

"Well that sounds good." They walked into the kitchen and Russell went to the stove and snitched a chunk of chicken.

"This smells delicious! What is it, chicken?"

"Yes Dad," Ginny sighed. *If only there was medication for this,* she thought.

"Why, I love chicken," Russell said as he walked into the dining room. Ginny picked up the bowl of vegetables and the potatoes and followed him to the table.

Russell sat down and, looking up at Ginny, said with his mouth still full, "I sure am hungry. Any chance we can have some dinner?"

"Dad, what's in your mouth?" Ginny showed a slight bit of irritation.

"Well, it tastes a lot like chicken."

"That's right." She left him to fetch the chicken from the kitchen.

"What are we having for dinner?" Russell hollered from his spot at the table.

Ginny drew in a deep breath. "Monkey brains, Dad."

*   *   *

That evening, Ginny opened the door and let in Edna and Russell's friend from church, Cordell Carey. "Thank you so much for coming over. I am at my wit's end. Their situation is hopeless unless we can convince Mother to take her lithium." Cordell walked into their living room and looked around for any of the Peaks. "Mother is the one taking care of the three of them, but unless she gets back under control, I'm not sure what to do anymore."

"Well, like I told you a few weeks ago on the phone, I've tried and tried, but to no avail."

"Maybe this time she'll listen. Who knows." Ginny had been praying and praying for help. She went to get Edna who was again in the hallway, poking the fishing rod into the attic opening.

"Someone's here to see you, Mother," Ginny informed her. Edna followed Ginny to the living room, still holding the fishing rod.

"What are you doing here?" Edna asked Cordell suspiciously.

"Edna, I'm here to tell you that you have no choice any more about taking your lithium." He didn't beat around the bush. "If you don't take it, starting today, I will have no choice but to take Russell and David out of the house and take them somewhere safe."

Edna glared at him, remaining silent. She let out a huge sigh and sat down in the overstuffed armchair next to the piano. She stared into the space in front of her, letting Cordell's ultimatum sink in. Ginny sat on the couch, waiting in suspense to hear what her mother was going to say, hoping, praying.

"You leave me no choice then," she finally mumbled. "I could never bear to have Russell or David taken away." Her shoulders drooped in defeat. "I'll take the lithium," she said as she fell further back into the chair in despair.

Ginny dropped down on her knees and threw her arms around her. "Thank you, Mother," she said tearfully.

Cordell reached out to Edna and put his hand on her shoulder. "Edna, I know this is hard. But I promise you that you are making the right choice, and everything will be alright." He handed her the prescription bottle. Ginny hurried into the kitchen for a glass of water. Edna took the medication.

Every day for a week Ginny handed Edna the pill and a glass of water and watched carefully as Edna swallowed it down. At the end of the week she and Edna were sitting outside in the backyard at the picnic table, eating lunch and talking.

"I'm so ashamed of myself. What a dear, dear daughter you are coming down here and *making* me do the right thing."

"Don't feel guilty, Mother. It's perfectly understandable for you to think that you would be alright going off your medication. I'm just so glad that we were able to convince you to take it again. Our prayers were answered for sure."

Just then, Ginny heard faint shouting coming from the house. It sounded like her Dad. She jumped up and ran through the back door, the screen slamming behind her. Sure enough, it was Russell, but he wasn't hurt, he was yelling at David. The TV was on and the two of them were engaged in a remote control war.

"David, I'm your father. Give that to me right now!" Russell hollered from his chair.

David stood in front of the TV, facing his father, holding tightly to the remote control. "NO!"

"Give it to me dammit!"

Ginny was dismayed at her father's language. For some reason, he not only had lost his memory abilities, he was also easily irritated and would get angry quickly, and sometimes curse. It was such a shame to see because he had been so kind and gentle his entire life.

Russell stood up, went to David and tried to grab the control from him. But David tightened his grip and yelled, "NO!"

Russell pulled and yanked. David pulled and yanked. Ginny couldn't help herself and started laughing hysterically. Both grown men, one 85 and the other 48, stopped their childish fight and looked over at Ginny. The anger faded from Russell's face and he asked, "What's so funny?"

"Oh Dad, YOU, fighting with David over a silly remote control."

Russell looked at David who continued to squeeze the remote control in his hand so tightly that his fingers were turning red.

"Why, no I wasn't," he said incredulously. He calmly walked back to his chair and sat back down. Looking again at David he said, "Davie dear, hand me that remote control, would you please."

David ignored his request and instead sat on the couch and began to flip through the channels.

"David, I said give me the remote control," Russell said, turning up the volume on his voice and adding some irritation.

David gave him the evil eye but said nothing and pointed the control at the TV.

"David, dammit! Give me the remote control!" Russell stood up and walked over to the couch and tried to grab the control from David's stubby Down Syndrome hand. David yanked back hard, causing Russell to lose his balance. He fell forward onto the couch, bounced off the back and rolled to the floor, narrowly missing the coffee table.

Ginny gasped and ran to him. "Dad, are you alright?"

Russell looked around. "Well, sure I am," he replied cheerfully. "But what the devil am I doing on the floor?"

39

June 1998

ALMOST A YEAR later, Jill walked into Bob and Ginny's house with 11-month-old Eliza on her hip. "Hi Grandma!" she said as she bent down and hugged Edna gingerly, who was sitting at the counter with a bowl of cereal in front of her.

"Hello Jill Darling!" Edna still had the same twinkle in her eye and adorable giggle that Jill remembered so well, but she looked amazingly different than the last time she had seen her. Ginny had described Edna to her, but she hadn't believed it until now. Edna had been plump for as long as Jill could remember, but now she was skin and bones. She had a bathrobe on because none of her clothes even remotely fit her anymore. Ginny had asked Jill to bring a few dresses with her for Edna to wear and looking at her now, even the ones she brought would probably be too big.

"Where's Grandpa and David?" Jill asked, turning to Bob.

"Grandpa's in our room taking a nap and David's still in the car. He won't come down the stairs because he's afraid of heights."

"You're kidding! Really?" Jill handed Eliza to Bob and started for the door. "I'll see if I can talk him into coming down with *me*."

"Ha! Good luck with Mr. Stubborn," Bob said under his breath as he tickled Eliza's chin.

Bob and Ginny had finally decided it was time to move Russell, Edna, and David to Montana to live with them. Edna had become too frail and arthritic to care for the three of them anymore. Russell had long since lost his ability to contribute to the overall care of the trio. He not only had the memory problem, but he was slow and walked tediously. He didn't really *walk*, he shuffled. He had worn a path, that looked like a cross country ski track, through their grassy lawn in the backyard of their Pasadena home by taking his daily "shuffle" around and around. Sometimes he would be out there for as long as an hour. Edna would call to him to come back inside, but he would insist that he had just barely begun his daily walk. When he finally reappeared, he would be covered head to toe in sweat. Edna would have to help him strip down, take a shower and redress. She just couldn't do it all anymore.

Bob and Ginny had retired and built their home on the lake in northern Montana. It was a beautiful and peaceful spot, but they had steep stairs leading from the driveway down to their front door, about 35 of them. Bob had simply scooped Edna up in his arms and carried her down, and Russell went down like a two-year old would – one step at a time. But David had refused to even attempt it. Or even get out of the car.

Knocking on the locked door, Jill hollered to David, "Davie! Open the door and give me a hug!" He looked at her through the window and smiled broadly. He unlocked the door, got out and gave Jill a hug.

"Jill…Jill…Jill," he echoed.

Jill took a good look at him. Like Edna, David had become thin and small. He had always been so chubby, it was a strange sight to see him so skinny. His face had become almost gaunt and his skin was wrinkled with age. But his hair was still dark, not a strand of grey hair to be found. Jill's hair had started to grey a bit as soon as she had turned 30 and David was almost 50 years old. *One of the benefits of Down Syndrome*, Jill thought.

"Come with me David. Ginny has yummy stuff to eat." Food would probably entice him, Jill hoped.

"Cake?" David asked with hope gleaming in his eyes.

"What, you want cake? Sure! Ginny has cake!" Jill lied.

"I like cake," David said as he rocked back and forth and ran a nervous hand through his hair.

Jill took his hand and led him to the gravel path that wound down towards the house, being careful to avoid the stairs. David grabbed her arm with both hands and started to dig his heals into the gravel in fear.

"It's alright David, really. You can do this. Just hold onto me and we'll get you into the house." *Boy if he goes down, we both go down*, Jill thought. *He is holding onto me so tightly I'm going to have fingerprints in my skin.*

David kept muttering, "No, no, no, no, no," and would occasionally pretend he was losing his balance.

But they finally made it down to the house and walked in the front door. "I did ith!" David announced.

Russell was standing in the kitchen, slightly hunched over and holding onto the counter for balance, but otherwise, Jill noticed immediately that he looked exactly the same. "Hi Grandpa!" she exclaimed as she came in and reached out to hug Russell.

He hugged her, patted her arm and sheepishly said, "Now, what's your name young lady?" Jill had been warned that he wouldn't remember who she was. He was down to Edna, David, Ginny, and Bob, but everyone else were just strangers.

"I'm Jill, Grandpa," she said, opening the cupboard and reaching for a *German Chocolate* cake mix box.

"Well, it's very nice to meet you dear."

40

September 2, 1998

J UST TWO MONTHS later Edna was dying. Bob and Ginny had purchased a comfortable little house close by for Edna, Russell, and David, and had hired a couple of nurses to help fill in the many hours of round-the-clock care that was needed for the three of them.

"I don't know what keeps her hangin' on, Mrs. Reed," one of the nurses said to Ginny in a quiet voice as she and Ginny looked down at Edna, who was lying in her bed, barely breathing. Continuing, the nurse said, "She *wants* to die, you can tell. She hasn't eaten or had anything to drink in five days. She's hanging on by a thread, but…" her voice trailed off as she shook her head. "Your dad comes in here several times a day and holds her hand and talks to her. She just stares at him. The rest of the time he shuffles around the house asking if anyone knows where his wife is."

"Has David come in to see her yet?" Ginny asked. David had refused to see his mother for the last two weeks. Ever since she had become bed-ridden he had stopped even talking about her.

"Not on my shifts. Not on Debbie's either. You could ask your daughters, but I don't think he has."

Ginny gazed down at Edna and quietly said, "I guess he just can't bear to see his mother this way. I don't blame him, it's very difficult for all of us."

"I've never seen anyone hang on at the very end like this before. Never." The nurse patted Edna on the shoulder and walked out to check on David and Russell.

Ginny sat down in a chair next to the bed and pulled out a letter from a box she was holding. "Mother, I found this box of letters at the house while we were packing everything. They are letters and notes that Dad wrote to you over the years. I thought you might enjoy it if I read some of them to you." Ginny looked over at Edna, who had actually moved her head a tiny bit to look at her. Ginny took it as a signal that she wanted the letters read to her. Clearing her throat and putting on her reading glasses, Ginny began to read:

My Darling Honey Girl,

I thought you might just like to know that you hold my heart in the palm of your lovely hand. You brighten my life more than the sun itself. I crave to see your smile and hear your adorable giggle. I know you would go with me to the end of the earth if you had to and not every man can say that. You are so smart, witty, fun-loving, and charming. My heart aches when you feel badly about yourself and I hope that one day you will see yourself the way I see you. The way God sees you. I know there will come a time when you will never feel sad again – ever. I'm so glad that I am your husband and will be by your side when that day comes. I'm not one much for a lot of words, so this is it for now. Forgive me for my weaknesses and love me, even if for the simple reason that I love you.

All my adoring love and affection,

Russell.

Ginny looked over at Edna, wondering if she was even able to understand, or even hear her. A tear trickled down Edna's cheek and onto the pillow. Ginny took a tissue and gently wiped Edna's damp cheek. "Shall I read another one Mother?" Again Edna gazed into Ginny's eyes, so Ginny took another small note card from the box and began to read it to Edna:

Good morning Sweetheart,
I found these lovely daisies on my walk this morning and they reminded me of your sweet cheerfulness. Have a most wonderful day,

Kisses,
Russell

Another note was pulled from the box:

Dear H. G.
I watched you sleep this morning and you are more Beautiful to me today than the day I married you.

Yours forever,
S.D.

Ginny knelt down next to the bed, tears trickling down her own cheeks. "Mother, it was a pleasure to grow up with parents who loved each other like you and Dad did." Ginny paused for a moment and continued, "You can go. Really. We all love you, Mother."

Deanna and Cherie had both come two weeks earlier, along with many of the grandchildren, to say their last good-byes. But Edna still clung to life.

She stared at Ginny, her mouth open, struggling for every breath. Ginny kissed her forehead and went into the kitchen to check on Russell and David. David was rocking back and forth on the couch, remote control in hand, watching TV. Russell was in the kitchen shuffling around the island, stopping after each lap at the cookie jar. "Oh, cookies. Why, I think I'll have one!" he said to himself as he took the lid off the jar, reached inside and took a cookie out. He ate the cookie as he shuffled another lap around the island, stopping at the cookie jar. "Oh, cookies! Why, I love cookies." Remove lid, reach inside, eat while shuffling. Another lap. Another cookie. Ginny watched until he had done about a dozen laps. He was back at the cookie jar, reaching inside. "I wonder who ate all the cookies," he said in dismay. "David, did you eat all the cookies?" he asked, a bit irritated.

David looked over from his program, his eyes wide. He stared at his Dad, not saying anything. Ginny intervened before her innocent brother got in trouble for something he didn't do. "Dad, Dad, David didn't eat any of them. *You* ate them all."

"I certainly did not!" he replied adamantly. "I haven't had a cookie all day."

Ginny sighed and went to the cupboard. She took out a large package of cookies and emptied them all into the cookie jar. "There Dad. Cookies. Have at it."

"Cookies! Why, I love cookies. Thank you darling." Russell took a bite and began to shuffle around the island again. Ginny wondered if a person could actually overdose on cookies.

*   *   *

Later that afternoon, as Ginny was watching TV with David, he suddenly got up from the couch and walked down the hall and into Edna's room. Ginny followed him and stood at the door, peeking in to see what he would do. David stood next to Edna's bed and gently stroked her hair. She looked up at him and smiled. He leaned over and kissed her cheek. Ginny was amazed and stood frozen, observing the tender scene. Edna reached up for him with her hand and he took her hand in his. "I love you Muthuh," he said and leaned down and kissed her again. He stood next to her bed for a long while, stroking her hair while she smiled up at her boy.

Time seemed to stand still and Ginny tried to cry quietly to herself so David wouldn't hear her. She didn't want him to see her, but she simply couldn't take her eyes off the most beautiful thing she had ever witnessed. All of the sudden he put Edna's hand back at her side and walked out of the room.

Fifteen minutes later Ginny went in to check on her mother. She was gone.

*   *   *

At the funeral home, Edna lay in her simple, yet lovely, cherry wood casket. Dressed in a white dress with flowers in her clasped hands, she looked beautiful, angelic, as if she where only sleeping. Bob and Ginny and the grandchildren living in Montana were all there. They had a simple memorial for her, casual and intimate. Ginny and Bob were taking her back to Pasadena the next day to be buried. Deanna and Cherie would meet them there.

Russell sat in a chair next to her. "She was a wonderful woman and a wonderful wife. I sure did love her. I don't know what I'll do without her." He gazed over at her every few minutes. Then he would talk some more about their life together, telling stories of how they met, vacations they had taken, holidays they had enjoyed, and trials they had endured. The family stayed for a while, listening, then finally said their goodbyes.

Walking down the steps of the funeral home, Russell turned to Ginny and asked, "Is this a funeral home?"

"Yes Dad."

"Who died?"

41

September 1998

RUSSELL LOOKED OVER at the pretty blond young woman sitting on the couch across the room from him. She had the most beautiful blue eyes, kind of like his. "Miss, do you know where my wife, Edna is?"

She came over to him and knelt at his knees, taking his hand in hers. "Oh, Grandpa, I'm so sorry to tell you, but Edna died a week ago." It was about the tenth time that day she had informed him of Edna's death.

Russell felt crushed. It pierced through him like a hot knife. He felt dizzy. How could she be gone from him? How could he live without her? Why couldn't he remember her being sick? And a whole week ago? How come no one had told him until now? He dropped his head into his hand and whimpered, "This is terrible." He reached into his pocket and shook out his perfectly folded, damp, handkerchief. Dabbing his eyes, he looked up at the TV. A McDonald's commercial was on. It sure did make him feel hungry.

"Miss, I sure do feel hungry. Do you think we could have some lunch now?"

Shawna looked up at him a little surprised. "We actually just had lunch Grandpa. Are you sure you *feel* hungry?"

"Well… are you sure we just ate?"

"Yes. I made you a big ham sandwich and chips and some potato salad."

"That sure sounds good! Is that what we're having for lunch?"

Shawna couldn't help but laugh at him. "Oh Grandpa, you are a corker." Somehow, that little bit of shuffling around the house and in the backyard that Russell did, managed to burn all the food he ate every day. He should be 300 pounds by now. But he hadn't changed a bit. She got up and went into the kitchen to serve him lunch – again.

As she handed him his plate full of food he looked up at her and asked, "Miss, do you know where my wife, Edna, is?"

Suddenly, David got up from his spot on the couch and shouted, "PASSTH AWAY! She passth away. Edna passth away." He glared at Russell in sheer annoyance. Russell looked back at him, wondering why he was so angry at him. He turned to Shawna and asked, "Miss, has my wife, Edna, passed away?"

Shawna decided to try something new and said very simply and matter-of-factly, "Yes, Grandpa, she did. I'm so sorry."

Russell hated to hear it, but somehow, he felt like he already knew it. "Oh, I was afraid of that." Russell hung his head and took a perfectly folded, damp, handkerchief from his pocket and dabbed his eyes, again. When he looked up there was a wonderful plate of food on his lap! "Lunch!" He looked up at Shawna and said, "Thank you dear. Did you make this for me?"

"Yes, Grandpa. I hope you enjoy it thoroughly." She sat down on the couch with David and put her arm around his shoulder.

Russell looked over at the pretty blond young woman sitting on the couch across the room from him and said, "I've forgotten your name, dear. What is it again?"

"Shawna. I'm one of Bob and Ginny's daughters."

"Oh! Well…" Russell looked right at her and thought for a moment. "That makes you my granddaughter, doesn't it!" This was wonderful. Russell felt so glad to have a beautiful granddaughter visiting him today. *And her eyes, they're just like mine*, he thought. He felt something in his hands and looked down to discover a big ham sandwich. He took a bite, chewed for a minute and swallowed. He looked up at the pretty young woman sitting on the couch across from him and asked, "Miss, do you know where my wife, Edna, is?"

42

1998-2001

TIME IS A funny thing. Sometimes it's on your side and sometimes it's your enemy. Sometimes it's both at the same time. As time went by it was Russell's friend because the torture of finding out that Edna had passed away, faded. He asked every day, all the time, for months on end. But as time passed, the answer became easier. Sometimes he could even figure it out himself if he was pushed.

"Well, Grandpa, what do you think?"

Russell would look down and think for a second, look up and say, "She passed away didn't she?"

"Yes, she did."

"That's what I thought."

But as time passed, Russell got older and older. He couldn't shuffle on his own anymore and needed the aid of a walker. His body began to fail, he had prostate cancer and he was prone to infections. He still ate about a dozen meals a day, mostly because he couldn't remember having just eaten. But the meals were getting smaller and smaller. One thing stayed the same – cookies. The cookie jar was emptied and refilled several times a day. Cookies were bought at Costco by the case. Ginny worried that under "cause of death" on his death certificate it would read: "Cookies."

No one would have thought that Russell ever even tried to keep track of time either. What was the point? But one day he asked David what day it was. David had always had an uncanny ability to know exactly what day of the week it was. No one had ever been able to provide any explanation for his unique ability, but it came in handy - especially when the family took their vacations and lost all track of what day it was.

Russell shuffled down the hall and came upon David watching TV.

"Davie dear, what day is it?"

David licked his lips and ran his hand through his hair. It took a lot out of him to think through something like this. He was aging too. He rocked back and forth for a minute and clacked his teeth to release his anxiety. He finally looked up at Russell and exclaimed, "Saturday!" and of course echoed, "Saturday...Saturday...Saturday."

~   Russell looked at him and asked, "What about Saturday?"

*   *   *

Christmas was an especially wonderful time. Everyone gathered at Bob and Ginny's house to open presents. One Christmas, Russell was handed a large, rather flat box. He opened it and exclaimed his pleasure upon finding a huge assortment of chocolates. He looked up and said to the group in general, "To whoever gave me these wonderful chocolates, thank you! I sure do love chocolates." He took one and popped it into his mouth as he replaced the box lid, then set the box down next to himself.

Just for fun, Bob decided to play with the memory-deprived Russell. "Here, Dad, I think this is for you," he said, handing Russell the box. Russell took the box and asked, "For me?" as he took the lid off. "My goodness! What a nice box of chocolates. To whoever gave me these, thank you."

"Why don't you have one Dad," Bob suggested.

"I think I will!" Russell said as he picked one out and popped it into his mouth.

A minute later, Bob handed him the box again. Russell was so pleased with his gift. "To whoever gave me this nice box of chocolates, thank you." He took another chocolate. Bob did the same trick a couple more times. Eventually, when Russell had opened the box again, half a dozen chocolates were missing. Bob pointed to the empty spaces and said, "Dad, look! Someone has already been into your chocolates and eaten some!" There were muffled giggles as everyone watched Russell's look of disappointment.

"Why look at that." Russell gazed down at the missing chocolates, dismayed. He looked up and asked, "Who ate my chocolates?"

Everyone cracked up. They couldn't help themselves. It was a welcome relief to laugh at something that was usually a frustration.

"What's so funny?" Russell asked with a smile appearing across his face. He wanted in on it.

Bob said, "Oh nothing Dad. Here, have a chocolate," and he handed him a morsel.

Russell popped it into his mouth and said, "Thank you to whoever gave me this nice box of chocolates!"

*   *   *

Time passed, but nothing changed. The family took turns looking after Russell and David, until Mother's Day, 2001, when Russell passed away peacefully in his sleep. It was a clear, beautiful Montana spring day. Perfect for fishing on the river.

43

April 27, 2002

IT WAS ZOE'S first birthday. She was Jill's fourth child, and the family was gathered to celebrate. David was sitting right next to her. Or more accurately, he was sitting right next to the cake. It was chocolate cake with pink frosting and purple gummy candies dotting the top. It looked adorable. David thought it looked delicious.

Since Edna and Russell had both passed away, David had been foot-loose and fancy free. Well, as much as a 53-year-old man with Down Syndrome can *be* foot-loose and fancy free. Bob and Ginny had sold the little house purchased for Edna, Russell, and David, and had moved David in with them.

Zoe was mesmerized by the purple candies and plucked them off, one at a time, popping them into her mouth and sucking all the sugar coating off and then spitting them out onto the table.

David pointed to the spit-out purple clumps and said, "Ginny, Ginny. She spit."

"I know David. It's okay."

David kept his eye on the cake. Everyone else kept their eye on Zoe. She was so cute with her big black eyes, long eyelashes and plump, pink lips. She was daintily touching her pretty pink cake.

Her siblings began to egg her on saying, "Eat your cake Zoe! Go ahead, take some!"

Zoe responded to the prodding by leaning over and taking a big bite right out of the edge of the cake. The kids cheered. David gasped. With pink frosting covering half her face, Zoe reached out and grabbed a huge chunk from the side and stuffed it into her mouth. Chocolate crumbs went flying and her big black eyes got wide as she stuffed the cake in. Everyone was giggling. David was panicking. But no one noticed.

Zoe went in for another handful. And another. And another. There was pink frosting dripped all over the table and chair and chocolate crumbs smeared on top of the pink frosting. It was in her hair, eyelashes and her ears. The kids egged her on even more. She stared at everyone for a moment, then stuffed her entire hand right down into the center of the cake and then squished it around in a circle. The family busted a gut. It was so cute.

But NOT to David. Amidst all the laughter, Ginny noticed poor, tortured David. He was pointing at the rapidly crumbling cake and hopelessly saying, "Jill, Jill, Jill. Cake. The cake." Then he wiped his face with his hands in anguish.

"Uh oh," Jill said, "I don't think David is too happy about this."

Everyone's attention turned to David. Zoe kept up with her demolition, but no one was watching her anymore. David was now stomping his feet and throwing his head around wildly in severe frustration. He pointed at the cake. "Look! Look what she doing." He was desperate to get anyone's help in saving the precious cake. Zoe's big black eyes looked straight at David as she took another giant handful. David was horrified. His eyes nearly popped out of his head. He stomped his feet some more and then put his head down on the table and pounded his fists next to his head in pure agony.

Finally, in David's moment of utter despair, God intervened. Zoe suddenly lost her balance on her chair. CRASH! Zoe fell off her chair, tipping the cake pedestal as she toppled. Jill scooped the screaming Zoe up and whisked her away. David stared at the remnants of what had been a perfectly good chocolate cake. He looked defeated. Ginny picked up what was left of the cake and asked for a knife. Miraculously, there was one thick, perfectly intact slice of chocolate cake with pretty pink frosting – just for David.

* * *

The years passed by. The families took David bowling, out for hamburgers and to church. Sometimes he spent the night at Jill's house or Shawna's house. He particularly loved that. Sometimes, when leaving Bob and Ginny's house, the departing family member would find a surprise in the front seat of their car – David.

"I spend the night your housth," he would say with hopeful eyes. Most of the time he got lucky. Other times Bob would have to come and wrestle him out of the car. David would grab hold of the door frame and his fingers would have to be plucked free one by one. Good thing he was so small, because he had a huge stubborn streak.

But aging started to set in and as with most Down Syndrome elderly individuals, David had Alzheimer's Disease. He started to forget faces. For everyone else except Ginny, he had an all-inclusive name: "Tricia." No one had any idea where he got the name. They didn't know any "Tricia." Even Sally seemed to have been forgotten. Eventually he became a recluse, staying in his room for days. It was such a sharp contrast to his stow-away days when he would do anything to go to someone's house. He didn't even want to go bowling anymore. Ginny would take his meals into him on a tray and watch TV with him for a while. She missed the days when David and Russell fought over the remote control. Occasionally, he would venture out of his room, usually just to make sure Ginny was there. He loved Ginny. So much.

But no one could get him to leave the house.

Epilogue

AVID LOOKED OUT the window. It was a beautiful day. The sky was bright blue and snow had fallen during the night and had laid a soft, downy covering on every tiny part of the world. The morning sun glistened off the ice crystals. It looked magical.

David's door opened and Ginny walked in with David's breakfast on a tray.

"Good morning Davie," he heard her say as she put the tray down on the table next to his sitting chair. He watched her as she went to the side of his bed.

"Davie?" she reached for him and gently shook his shoulder. "David!" she repeated a little louder. He could hear her just fine, but there was nothing he could do. He could see himself, lying there, completely still.

Ginny stood next to him and put her hands to her mouth as she gasped. She leaned over his body, hugged him tightly, and wept. David continued to watch her and heard her finally say, "I love you little brother. You can be with Mother and Dad now," she said through her tears.

He stayed for a moment longer and watched as Ginny called for Bob, who came quickly into the room. Realizing what had happened, Bob knelt down at the side of the bed and held Ginny in his arms as she cried.

Feeling that everything would be properly taken care of, David left the room, and the house.

*   *   *

David found himself quite suddenly in a very bright field. At first he had to squint his eyes to focus on anything, but it didn't take long until his eyes adjusted to the light and he looked out over the most beautiful field of flowers he had ever seen. They came up almost to his waist and were the most vibrant colors, and so many colors! Even colors he couldn't recall having ever seen before. He began to walk straight ahead, brushing the tops of the flowers with his hand held out from his side.

In the distance, he could see a magnificent tree. The trunk was white, the foliage was several shades of bright green. The branches twisted, turned, and bent in all directions, and was taller than anything near it. It was majestic. It was elegant. David continued to walk toward the resplendent tree.

As he came closer, he noticed people, many, many people, gathered in clusters around and near the tree. He felt drawn to it, almost a part of it. As he continued toward the tree, he saw two people walking toward him. As they approached him, David stood still.

"Oh David! My darling, darling David!" the woman exclaimed.

Suddenly David knew her. "Mother!" he shouted as he threw his arms around her. It was the most wonderful hug, it didn't feel exactly like his body was feeling the hug, it was more like his soul felt the hug. He had missed his mother so much.

David pulled away from her and looked at the handsome, young man with brilliant blue eyes next to her. "Dad!" he said as he put his arms around his father's shoulders in a manly embrace.

The three of them stood together and hugged each other in the most joyous reunion. Finally, Edna gently pushed David slightly away and said, "Now, let us get a good look at you." She and Russell both inspected their son.

Russell put his arm on David's shoulder and said, "Look how tall you are, David! I guess all that wishing on your birthdays finally paid off."

"I always felt a little squished in that short body," David laughed.

"You're the most handsome young man." Edna said with a radiant smile. "You always have been."

"I hardly recognized the two of you!" David said with a grin. "Mother, you look beautiful. I'd forgotten what your hair looked like brown. It's lovely. And Dad, I didn't even know you ever *had* hair!" David said as he patted the top of Russell's thick blond hair.

David looked at his father in a white short-sleeved shirt and white pants and commented, "Dad, why don't you have a tie on? I have one."

Russell reached up and tightened David's tie a tiny bit and answered, "Ties are optional here, but they said you would really love to wear one."

David puffed his chest out slightly and stroked his hand down the white, silk tie. "They were right. I love it."

Edna took his hand in both of hers and said, "There's someone who is especially anxious to meet you." She guided him closer to the tree until they came upon a woman who was quite petite and had long brown hair and brown eyes. "David darling, this is my mother, Gertrude."

"Hello David. I've heard so very much about you," she said as she reached her arms up and around his neck to hug him. "You were a shining star of comfort and love to your mother and father," she smiled up at him. She had a twinkle in her eye and a soft giggle. David thought it remarkable how much *his* mother was like *her* mother.

"It is a wonderful day to finally be with you as well, Grandmother."

"David," Edna said, taking David by the arm and gesturing to the man standing next to Gertrude, "You remember my father, don't you?"

"Grandpa!" David hugged him tightly. "Of course I remember you. You came over and helped take care of me all the time. I just... didn't recognize you. You look so..."

"Young?" Grandpa Ledyard offered.

"Well, yes. You're all young," David said, looking around the group. "The last time I saw you Mother and Dad, you were old."

"You were no spring chicken yourself there, David! By the end, you were 60!" Russell teased, then turned to the man and woman standing just off to his side. "You remember my parents don't you son?"

"Grandma! Grandpa!" The three embraced. "Wow! This is the best day of my life! David whooped.

"Your *afterlife*," Edna corrected him with her signature giggle that he had missed for so many years.

"OK. Now, come with me." Russell began to lead the group past the great tree. They walked a short distance, reminiscing together as they walked. Nothing took any effort here, David noticed. He felt so strong. Talking was wonderful! His tongue was so small, and it was easy to form words. He felt as if he could just talk and talk and talk.

The group came to a most glorious lake with water in shades of blue, emerald, turquoise and even lavender. It was the most beautiful sight David had ever seen. Trees of all different varieties and colors lined the shores and rocks looked like they glistened.

"David, look at yourself," Russell said, pointing to the water. "There are no mirrors here, but you can see yourself in the reflection."

David peered down at the crystal-like water. He could make out a man with brown hair and brown eyes, tall and thin. He looked the same as he always had, but just a little different, and young again. He straightened his tie and ran his hands through his hair. Turning to the group he said, "I like it."

*   *   *

David sat on an elegant, white marble bench with his mother and father. They gazed out across the wide expanse of wildflowers. They had strolled for a while around the lake, taking all the time they wanted, returning eventually to the great tree where David was introduced to more relatives. They were all so happy to meet him. He could remember all their names – he had perfect recall. It was an odd feeling to remember everything, new things, old things, anything. He had instant understanding of anything someone explained to him.

David ran his hand across intricate carvings of figs and vines on the marble bench. He wanted to ask his mother and father something, but hesitated, not sure if he wanted to know the answer. Finally, he turned to them and asked, "Were you disappointed when I was born?"

Russell's blue eyes looked softly at his son as he reached over and put a hand on David's shoulder. "We didn't understand so many things when you were born. But, in time, you became the most joyful blessing of our lives."

Edna reached for David's arm and squeezed it. "Because of you, I had a much healthier mind than I would have had if you hadn't been born just as you were. You were a real comfort to me so very many times. You made me try harder."

"But I know I was also very difficult, annoying, stubborn – "

Edna cut off David's list. "You were charming, adorable, thoughtful, funny, kind, helpful, loving, affectionate, and as dear a boy as a mother could ever hope for."

"You forgot humble," David quipped.

As they laughed together, David noticed a young woman with long blond hair walking toward them. She was looking straight at David, and only at David. Russell and Edna suddenly excused themselves and rose to leave.

"Wait, Mother, Dad, don't go yet."

But Edna simply patted his knee, smiled at him, and walked off with Russell, leaving David alone on the bench.

"Hello David," the girl said with a soft, sweet smile, her blue eyes sparkling in the light.

An energy surged through David's whole being. He jumped off the bench.

"Sally!"

*   *   *

David and Sally walked side by side through the vast meadow of wildflowers. David glanced over at Sally and marveled at her beauty. He couldn't believe she was right there, next to him again. Her hair was flowing behind her in the gentle breeze and she looked perfectly angelic in a light pink dress that swayed with the wind.

"I'm sorry I forgot you," David finally said, looking over at her.

"That's alright. I knew you eventually would. It was inevitable. But it doesn't even matter now, does it?"

They came to an overlook and sat down together under a beautiful bright red tree.

"Everything here is..." David couldn't quite think of how he wanted to describe what he was feeling about it all.

"Perfect?" Sally offered.

"Yes. Perfect." David reached down and plucked up a blueish colored flower. "Every flower, every leaf, every cloud, every tree. There are no flaws, in anything at all." David gazed out over the valley below. "It looks so much like earth, only…"

"Perfect?" Sally repeated.

"You look perfect." David tucked the flower behind Sally's ear. Sally smiled sweetly at him.

Pointing to the deep valley below Sally said, "Look, do you see the animals?"

David focused on the area she was pointing to. "Oh, yes, I see them." He looked for a while and then noticed something quite remarkable. "Wow! I see elephants, tigers, cows, dogs, lambs, lions. All together. None of them are fighting, or chasing, or eating each other!" David stared at the animals in wonder.

Sally laughed and said, "Of course they're not! They're all friends. They talk to each other."

David looked at Sally with wide eyes. Surely, she was pulling his leg. "They do?"

"Yes, they do," Sally said completely matter-of-factly.

David continued watching the animals, then asked, "Are there snakes here? Mother hates snakes."

"Snakes?" Sally looked surprised at the question. "Of course there's no snakes here."

"Oh, good. I'm sure my mother was very happy about that."

"Speaking of snakes, you owe me, you know."

David looked at her, confused, trying to figure out what she could possibly be talking about.

"You don't remember, do you?"

David shook his head, "No, apparently not."

"Your memory will all come back little by little." Sally explained further, "When you were just a little boy, about a year and half old, you wandered away from your campsite. You sat down in a road, right next to a poisonous snake."

David looked down, searching his mind until he came to something about a snake. He closed his eyes, trying to remember. Then, a memory played in his head, almost like a movie. "I remember now! And I touched it." David looked at Sally in shock at the memory. "I thought it was a toy. But for some reason... David squinted as he tried to remember more. He looked back up at Sally. "You were there. You told the snake not to bite me."

Sally grinned at him. "You owe me."

"You saved my life."

"Many times, my friend." Sally threw her head back and gave a hearty laugh. "You were so mischievous. I had to get others to help me a few times. Like the horses. That took a few of us."

"The horses?" David again tried to remember.

"Yes, the horses, at the ranch in Montana. And let's not forget New Year's Day. You really should have obeyed your mother. And I couldn't believe you tried to blame it on *me*!" she laughed.

It was all starting to come back to him. He looked over at Sally. "You were there with me... all the time."

"I was there as much as I could be. Towards the end, it made me so sad that you didn't even know me anymore that I stayed here and waited for you."

"I'm sorry, Sally." David reached down and took her hand in his. They sat in the silence for a long time. Birds, of all different varieties, flew overhead. The light stayed steady and constant. David didn't feel hungry or tired. He could spend forever there, with Sally. It was like a dream. But so much better. It was real. It was Heaven.

*　　*　　*

"Do you know why I was born with Down Syndrome?" David asked Sally one day.

"Well, yes. Don't *you* know?"

"I know I was born to bless my mother and father's lives. And my sisters."

"Yes, that's true. But there's more. Most people go to earth to gain experience, to learn and to figure out how to treat other people. Some prove that they love others, and some prove that they are selfish. Some people are so special they don't need to prove anything. So, God sends them in a type of body that is protected, so to speak, from being bad. They *can't* really ever be bad. It's like they stay an innocent child their whole lives. You were one of them."

"Why did I have to go at all then?"

"Everyone has to go silly. But this way, God made it so that you would *for sure* come back here – to Heaven."

David thought about what Sally said for a long time. She had a way of explaining things that always made him feel warm and happy inside. She was always so bright and cheerful. He loved her.

"I have a surprise for you," Sally said, bringing him back from his thoughts.

Sally handed David a fishing rod. "Your dad is waiting for you at the river," Sally beamed at David.

David took the rod in his hands. "Where did you get this?"

"I thought it, and it was," Sally shrugged, not sure of how to explain something that she did all the time so easily.

"Well, gosh. Fishing with my dad!" David could hardly stand the excitement. "There's fishing here?"

"Your dad said it was something called 'catch and release.' But your dad is excited to show you how to use that thing," Sally said, pointing to the fishing rod. "He said he's going to show you all his 'casting tricks,' whatever that means."

David suddenly turned from Sally and bounded away, fishing rod in hand, shouting, "Thanks Sally!" As he ran farther away from her, she saw a white tie thrown into the wind.

*   *   *

Russell and Edna were waiting under a beautiful Shady tree by the side of a glorious river. They were laughing and eating chocolates from a large white box.

"Hi Mother, hi Dad," David said cheerfully as he approached them. Then he spied the chocolates. "You can *eat* here?"

"Oh yes!" said Edna. "It's one of the best things about it. So enjoyable. And you don't get fat!" She lifted the box to offer one to David. "Have one. They're wonderful."

"Is there cake here too?" David asked as he took a chocolate from the box and sat down.

Edna and Russell had to laugh. "Yes, son. Whatever flavor you would like." Russell began to laugh harder and continued, "We felt so sorry for you when Zoe destroyed her cake right in front of you. We knew it was pure torture for you. However, your little temper tantrum was so funny."

"You *saw* that?" David said, a little ashamed. "I wouldn't act that way now, you know."

"Oh son, it's alright. Everything's alright," Russell said as he looked out over the river. "What do you say we go fishing?"

"Oh boy! Dad, this is the best surprise!"

"I thought seeing Sally again was the best surprise," giggled Edna, grinning at David. "It was the best surprise for *us*, when we got here."

"Well…" David began, shifting his weight and smiling. "Well, I guess this is the second-best surprise then." He turned to Russell and said, "You first, Dad. I'll follow you."

Russell waded into the river, his son following behind him.

"David, I have to go," Sally said one day as she listened to David play the violin. He played so beautifully. She could spend hours listening to him.

"Go where?" David asked nonchalantly, still playing softly.

"To earth."

David's fingers suddenly stopped moving along the fingerboard. He took the violin out from under his chin and his arms dropped to his side, violin in one hand, bow in the other. "To earth?" David felt like he could hardly say the words. "But you can't leave. It feels like I just got here. Sally, please. Please, stay here. With me."

"Actually, you've been here for the same as five earth years," Sally tried to comfort him.

"Yes, but time just feels so different here."

"I know. But I won't be gone long." Sally reached up and touched David's cheek. She could see an expression of sadness come over his face.

David fiddled with the strings on his violin, plucking them absentmindedly while he thought about how much he would miss Sally. "What if…" David could hardly say what he was thinking. "What if you don't come back?"

"I will," Sally said with confidence.

"Promise me Sally. Oh, promise me." David put his violin down and took Sally's hands in his.

With tears brimming in her eyes Sally quietly said, "I promise you," and lifted David's hand to her soft, tear-stained cheek.

* * *

Mike held tight to Vida's hand, "You can do it honey. Just one more big push."

Vida pushed as hard as she could, squeezing her eyes shut and gripping Mike's hand so hard he thought she'd break his fingers.

There was a cry that filled the delivery room and Vida lay back onto the bed with relief, drawing in deep, satisfying breaths of air.

Mike kissed her cheek and said, "You did it. You were amazing!"

"It's a girl," the doctor announced.

But rather than handing the baby immediately to Vida, the doctor and nurses took the baby over to the warmer and huddled around her.

"What's wrong? Is something wrong," Mike said with concern as he went over to the warmer and tried to see what was going on. The baby was pink and wailing as the doctor put a stethoscope to her chest. "Her lungs seem fine," Mike said in an attempt to ease some of the stress. No one said anything as they continued to examine the baby.

"Mike," Vida called out, "Mike is she okay? Someone please tell me what's going on."

Mike went back to Vida and held her hand. Finally, the doctor came to their side and said they were going to take the baby down the hall to the nursery for a moment and they'd be back as quickly as possible.

Vida began to cry in Mike's arms while he tried to comfort her. "She was crying and pink and flailing her arms. I'm sure she's fine," Mike said as he stroked Vida's hair and brushed away her tears.

Vida and Mike waited. After 20 long minutes, the doctor reappeared along with a nurse who was holding a tiny bundle, wrapped like a burrito in a pink blanket and her head in a pink and blue striped hospital beanie. She gently handed the pink burrito to Vida who sobbed in relief as she gazed down for the first time at her new daughter.

The doctor gave them a few moments then spoke to them in a gentle voice, "Mike and Vida, your baby has a heart condition called atrioventricular septal defect, or ASD. Put simply, she has at least one hole in her heart that most likely will need to be repaired as soon as she is strong enough to go through surgery, typically by the time she is about six to nine months old."

"Oh my gosh. This sounds really bad," said Vida with grave concern.

"Well, it's actually somewhat common in babies like yours," the doctor paused as Mike and Vida both looked at him with alarm.

"Babies like ours?" Mike repeated.

"Your baby has Down Syndrome," the doctor said gently.

Mike and Vida looked at each other, then at their precious new daughter. A tear fell on top of her pink and blue striped beanie as Vida held her even closer. Mike leaned down and whispered, "You're perfect. We love you," and he pressed his cheek against her forehead, then kissed her soft, chubby, pink cheek.

Mike and Vida cried, and laughed, and hugged their new daughter.

Looking at Vida, Mike said, "Let's name her Sally."

Edna at the University of Minnesota, 1932.

Russell, 1931.

Edna with newborn David.

Edna and David around 8 months old.

David age 3 in the side yard
of their Pasadena, California home.

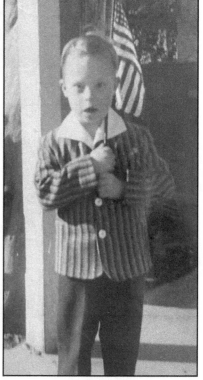

David, 5 years old.

David receiving his gold medal for swimming
at the 1970 Special Olympics.

Edna's painting of Russell fishing in Montana, 1966.

PEAK'S RIFFLE ON ALLEN RIVER

One of many drawings Ken
Anderson did of Russell.

Letter from one of Russell's
customers.

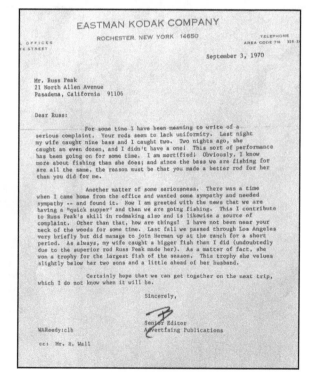

EASTMAN KODAK COMPANY

ROCHESTER, NEW YORK 14650

September 3, 1970

Mr. Russ Peak
21 North Allen Avenue
Pasadena, California 91106

Dear Russ:

For some time I have been meaning to write of a
serious complaint. Your rods seem to lack uniformity. Last night
my wife caught nine bass and I caught two. Two nights ago, she
caught an even dozen, and I didn't have a one! This sort of performance
has been going on for some time. I am mortified! Obviously, I know
more about fishing than she does; and since the bass we are fishing for
are all the same, the reason must be that you made a better rod for her
than you did for me.

Another matter of some seriousness. There was a time
when I came home from the office and wanted some sympathy and needed
sympathy -- and found it. Now I am greeted with the news that we are
having a "quick supper" and then we are going fishing. This I contribute
to Russ Peak's skill in rodmaking also and is likewise a source of
complaint. Other than that, how are things? I have not been near your
neck of the woods for some time. Last fall we passed through Los Angeles
very briefly but did manage to join Herman up at the ranch for a short
period. As always, my wife caught a bigger fish than I did (undoubtedly
due to the superior rod Russ Peak made her). As a matter of fact, she
won a trophy for the largest fish of the season. This trophy she values
slightly below her two sons and a little ahead of her husband.

Certainly hope that we can get together on the next trip,
which I do not know when it will be.

Sincerely,

Senior Editor
Advertising Publications

WAReedy:clh

cc: Mr. R. Wall

"If there's no fishing in Heaven,
I'd prefer to go elsewhere."

~ RUSSELL PEAK

O Promise Me

Lyrics by Clement Scott
Music by Reginald DeKoven

Oh, promise me that someday you and I
Will take our love together to some sky.
Where we can be alone and faith renew
And find the hollows where those flowers grew.
Those first sweet violets of early spring,
Which come in whispers, thrill us both,
And sing of love unspeakable that is to be.
Oh promise me! Oh promise me!

Promise me that you will take my hand,
The most unworthy in this lonely land.
And let me sit beside you, in your eyes
Seeing the vision of our paradise,
Hearing God's message while the organ rolls
It's mighty music to our very souls;
No love less perfect than a life with thee.
Oh promise me! Oh promise me!

Acknowledgements

To my children, Jessica, Isaac, Eliza, Zoe, Allie, Addison, Julia, Jonathan, Benjamin, and Will, who all encouraged me and told me endlessly that I could do anything. During the months of writing this book, they found things to do, and I would hear them say to each other, "Shhh, Mom's writing her book." I love you all with my whole soul.

To my mother Ginny, who read every chapter practically the minute I was finished writing it. Her opinion was of paramount importance to me, and I still recall nervously handing her the first chapter, afraid that she wouldn't like it. When she handed the pages back, with tears in her eyes she said that she loved it. I miss you Mom.

To my father Robert (Bob), who proofread every chapter, twice. If it weren't for him, I would make ghastly grammatical errors such as, "Me and so-and-so" rather than "So-and-so and me," and I might not know the difference between "your" and "you're." I'm sorry I still get *lay* and *lie* wrong Dad. I promise I will continue to teach my children proper English now that you are gone from us.

The first person I gave the manuscript to who was not a family member, was Jerry Molen. I was so nervous about it I nearly fainted.

I will forever be in his debt for taking time between movie projects to read it. It has been my privilege and honor to utilize his opinion and advice and to have his quote on the cover. Jerry, you and Pat are the finest example to me of lovely, gracious, genuine people and I thank you for helping bring this book to fruition.

I am very grateful for my dear friend and acting editor, Kristin Kerr, who read the manuscript years ago when I first finished it, and then again this year. There were things that I never would have realized or thought of without her insight, wisdom, and honesty. Kristin, thank you for your sweet voice, your patient heart, your honest opinion, and most of all your friendship.

To my cover designer, Glen Edelstein, who nailed it on the first try and I was too inexperienced to realize it. He had incredible patience with me as he humored me through some of my ideas (that weren't good.) Glen, I am grateful for your experience in the book industry and for your care in creating a beautiful cover. "You can't judge a book by the cover" may be true, and yet…. It's the first thing a reader sees!

Finally, I am eternally grateful to Edna and Russell for living life the way they did – lovingly, kindly, gently; for their industry and hard work; for their example of devotion and loyalty, tenacity, and perseverance. I was incredibly blessed to read Edna's journals, something she most likely never thought were anything special. Now all who read this book can see how special she was, along with Russell, David, Virginia, Deanna, and Cheryl. They were truly remarkable. I love you all and hope the family reunions spoken of in the epilogue will one day be a lovely reality where I can bask in your presence and hear you call me "Jill Darling" once again.

Author's Note

SOME HAVE ASKED me why I chose to end the book the way I did – the body of the book having been true stories, the epilogue obviously fictitious. My answer is this: I knew the Peaks very well; Edna and Russell were my grandparents, David my uncle, and Ginny was my mother. One of the things that was their hope and guide throughout their lives, was the assurance that they would be together after death, together with all their generations of family, and that David would then be made perfect: his "mask of Down Syndrome" as they referred to it, would be removed and they would have the honor and pleasure of seeing him without that mask. They spoke of that future occasion many times and looked forward to it. They also theorized about Sally and wondered if she was in fact real – just unseen to the rest of them. They hoped she was, and always spoke about her to David as if she was. I know they would not only be pleased with this ending, but would have felt the book incomplete without it.

~ Jill Delee Reed

About the Author

JILL DELEE REED began writing when she was asked to be a regular columnist for the local newspaper and for nearly two years she wrote "Jill's Jabber," a humorous and down-to-earth glimpse at raising her 10 children. She lives in Bigfork, Montana, has two grandsons, two dogs, and absolutely hates snakes.

Find the author on:

And at:
www.jilldeleereed.com

CPSIA information can be obtained
at www.ICGtesting.com
Printed in the USA
FSHW010536240921
84983FS